JUST ESSAYS

101

Must Read
Argumentative Essays

#NONONSENSE
#theonlyargumentativeessaybookyouneed

-Michael Shin-

**Suitable for students sitting for
IELTS or TOEFL**

While every precaution has been taken in the preparation of this book, the publisher assumes no responsibility for errors or omissions, or for damages resulting from the use of the information contained herein.

JUST ESSAYS 101 ARGUMENTATIVE ESSAYS

First edition. February 19, 2023.

ISBN: 979-8215653258

Written by Michael Shin.

Table of Contents

What is this book about?

Writing a good argumentative essay can be a challenging task, especially for students preparing for exams like IELTS and TOEFL. As an experienced English teacher, I have witnessed numerous students struggling to write well-structured and effective argumentative essays. I have also seen how expensive study materials and guides can be, which can limit access to quality resources for students in need. That's why I decided to compile this book of 101 argumentative essays.

My goal is to provide students with a comprehensive guidebook that is accessible to everyone, regardless of their financial situation. This book includes a variety of essay topics and is designed to help students develop their argumentative writing skills at their own pace. Each essay is accompanied by an analysis of its structure and content, providing readers with a clear understanding of how to construct a successful argumentative essay easily.

I hope that this book will be a valuable resource for all students who are preparing for exams or who simply want to improve their writing skills. By providing a wide range of examples, I aim to help readers gain the exposure and confidence they need to succeed. I believe that this book will inspire readers to approach their writing with more creativity and confidence, and that it will help them achieve the success they deserve.

What are some of the key criteria that examiners use to assign a band 9 score for IELTS Task 2 essays, and how does the model answer described in the passage meet those criteria?

In a Band 9 score for Task 2 of the IELTS exam, the examiner sees

- a **comprehensive response that fully addresses the question** by presenting various arguments **for and against a topic.**

- the writer's **stance is clear and communicated effectively in the conclusion.**

- the writing style is **suitable for academic writing** and the essay is **at least 250 words in length.**

- the **coherence and cohesion** of the essay are **noteworthy**, with **well-organized paragraphs** and **logical links between ideas.**

- the essay demonstrates **a good range of vocabulary**, including natural collocations, and utilizes reporting and hedging verbs to strengthen the arguments.

- the grammatical range and accuracy are also commendable, with **the use of various grammatical structures** appropriate for academic writing, **without any grammatical errors**.

MICHAEL SHIN

General Structure of Some Argumentative Essays

The Death Penalty: An Inhumane and Ineffective Punishment

INTRO

Current issue   *Stance*

The use of the death penalty has been a controversial issue for decades. While some argue that it is a necessary form of punishment for the most heinous crimes, others maintain that it is an inhumane and ineffective way of dealing with crime. This essay will argue that the death penalty is not only morally wrong, but also fails to achieve its intended goals of deterrence and justice. *Your View*

BODY

Main Point/Argument supporting one of the stances

Firstly, the death penalty is morally wrong. The taking of a human life, regardless of the circumstances, is a grave injustice. It goes against the basic human right to life and the dignity of human beings. It also creates a cycle of violence and retribution that can never be justified. Moreover, the death penalty is often applied in a discriminatory manner, with poor and marginalized communities being disproportionately affected. This is a clear violation of human rights and social justice.

Relevant supporting ideas

Main Point/Argument supporting the same stance

Secondly, the death penalty fails to achieve its intended goals of deterrence and justice. Studies have consistently shown that the death penalty does not deter crime any more effectively than other forms of punishment, such as life imprisonment. In fact, some research has suggested that the death penalty may even increase violent crime by sending a message that violence is an acceptable way to solve problems. Additionally, the death penalty has been shown to be prone to error, with innocent people sometimes being sentenced to death. This undermines the credibility of the justice system and perpetuates the cycle of injustice. *Relevant supporting ideas*

Main Point/Provide alternatives or solutions

Finally, there are more effective alternatives to the death penalty that can achieve the same goals of justice and deterrence without resorting to violence. One such alternative is life imprisonment without the possibility of parole. This ensures that dangerous criminals are removed from society while also allowing for the possibility of rehabilitation and reintegration. Furthermore, a focus on addressing the root causes of crime, such as poverty, inequality, and lack of access to education and healthcare, can also help to reduce crime rates and promote a more just and peaceful society. *Relevant supporting ideas*

Review all the main points

In conclusion, the death penalty is an inhumane and ineffective form of punishment that violates basic

CONCLUSION human rights and perpetuates a cycle of violence and retribution. There are more effective alternatives that can achieve the same goals without resorting to violence. It is time for us to abandon the death penalty and work towards a more just and peaceful society.

Leave the reader with an interesting thought

General Structure
of Some Argumentative Essays

Title

The Pros and Cons of Homework: Does It Actually Help Kids?

INTRO

General issue   *Stance*

Homework has been a long-standing tradition in education, but in recent years, there has been a debate on its effectiveness. Some argue that homework is essential in helping children learn and succeed academically, while others believe that it does not provide any significant benefits and may even be detrimental to a child's mental and physical health. In this essay, we will explore both sides of the argument and determine whether homework actually helps kids.

Your View

BODY

Main Point/Argument supporting one of the stances

Those who advocate for homework argue that it reinforces classroom learning, helps develop study habits and time management skills, and prepares children for the demands of higher education and the workforce. Homework provides an opportunity for children to review and practice what they have learned in class, and to identify areas where they may need additional help. Additionally, homework can help develop critical thinking and problem-solving skills, as students are required to apply their knowledge to complete assignments.

Main Point/Argument supporting the opposite stance

On the other hand, opponents of homework argue that it can have negative effects on children's mental and physical health, and may not actually improve academic performance. Some studies have shown that excessive homework can lead to sleep deprivation, stress, and anxiety, and may even contribute to the development of conditions such as depression. Furthermore, some argue that homework can be an unfair burden on children from low-income families who may not have access to the same resources as their more affluent peers.

Main Point/Justification

If you are sitting for IELTS, this paragraph is optional. Write only if you have the time.

Despite the arguments on both sides, the evidence on the effectiveness of homework is mixed. Some studies have found a positive correlation between homework and academic performance, while others have found no significant correlation or even a negative one. Additionally, some studies have found that the amount and type of homework can make a difference - for example, shorter assignments and projects that encourage creative thinking may be more effective than lengthy rote assignments.

Review all the main points

CONCLUSION

The bottom line is this. The question of whether homework helps kids is a complex one, and there is no definitive answer. It may have some benefits in terms of reinforcing learning and developing skills, but it may also have negative effects on children's health and well-being. As educators and parents, it is important to consider the individual needs and circumstances of each child when deciding whether to assign homework, and to ensure that any homework assigned is appropriate, effective, and not overly burdensome.

Leave the reader with an interesting thought

Balancing the Benefits and Drawbacks of Technology: Navigating the Impact on Society

The rapid advancements in technology have significantly impacted the way we live and work. Some argue that technology has improved the quality of life, while others believe it has caused more harm than good. In this essay, I will argue that although technology has brought many benefits to society, its negative effects cannot be ignored and need to be addressed.

On the one hand, technology has made life easier and more convenient. For instance, people can now communicate with each other from anywhere in the world through social media and instant messaging. This has made it possible to maintain relationships with friends and family members who live far away, and has also allowed people to collaborate on projects more efficiently. Additionally, technology has revolutionized the way we access information, with the internet providing a wealth of knowledge at our fingertips.

However, there are also significant downsides to the increased use of technology. One major concern is the impact it is having on our mental health. The constant exposure to screens and social media can lead to anxiety, depression, and sleep problems. Furthermore, there is evidence to suggest that technology is also affecting our ability to form meaningful relationships and connect with others in real life. Many people now spend more time online than they do interacting with their family and friends, which can lead to feelings of loneliness and social isolation.

Another negative effect of technology is the loss of privacy. With the increasing amount of personal information that is shared online, there is a greater risk of data breaches and identity theft. In addition, many tech companies use personal data to target advertising and influence our behaviour, which some see as a violation of privacy.

All in all, technology has brought many benefits to society, but its negative effects cannot be ignored. It is important that we find ways to mitigate these negative impacts and ensure that technology is used in a responsible and ethical manner. This may involve setting limits on screen time, developing new privacy laws, and investing in research to better understand the impact of technology on our mental and physical health. By doing so, we can ensure that technology continues to improve our lives, rather than making them worse.

Artificial Intelligence

The rise of automation and artificial intelligence (AI) has led to widespread concerns about job loss and economic displacement. Some argue that automation will free up workers from dangerous and repetitive tasks, allowing them to pursue more fulfilling careers. Others believe that automation will lead to widespread unemployment, as machines take over jobs that were once performed by humans. In this essay, I will argue that while automation has the potential to cause significant job loss, it also presents an opportunity for workers to acquire new skills and transition to new industries.

On the one hand, automation has the potential to significantly disrupt the job market. Many routine and manual tasks, such as assembly line work and data entry, are at risk of being taken over by machines. This could lead to widespread unemployment, as workers are displaced from their jobs and struggle to find new employment. This, in turn, could lead to economic hardship, as people struggle to make ends meet without a steady source of income.

However, there is also the argument that automation can lead to a reallocation of labour and an increase in productivity. As machines take over routine tasks, workers will be freed up to focus on more creative and fulfilling work. Additionally, the transition to a more automated economy could create new jobs in industries such as software development, data analysis, and maintenance of automation systems.

Furthermore, automation presents an opportunity for workers to acquire new skills and transition to new industries. In order to remain competitive in the job market, workers will need to adapt to the changing landscape and develop new skills, such as coding and data analysis. This could lead to a more educated and skilled workforce, which in turn could drive economic growth and innovation.

In conclusion, while automation has the potential to cause significant job loss, it also presents an opportunity for workers to transition to new industries and acquire new skills. It is important that governments and organizations take steps to address the negative effects of automation, such as providing support for workers who are displaced from their jobs, and investing in education and training programs to help people transition to new careers. By doing so, we can ensure that the rise of automation is a positive development for workers and the economy as a whole.

Examining the Impact of Cell Phones on Our Lives

The widespread use of cell phones has been a topic of much debate in recent years. On the one hand, proponents argue that cell phones have greatly improved our lives by providing instant access to information and connecting us with friends and family. On the other hand, critics argue that cell phones have had negative impacts on our health and social interactions. In this essay, I will examine both sides of the argument and come to a conclusion about the overall impact of cell phones on our lives.

In terms of the positive impact of cell phones, it is undeniable that they have revolutionized the way we communicate and access information. With just a few taps on our screens, we can send messages, make calls, and access a wealth of knowledge on the internet. This has made it easier than ever to stay connected with people, even when we are far apart. Additionally, cell phones have allowed people to access information and services, such as banking and healthcare, from anywhere, at any time. Moreover, cell phones have become a valuable tool for emergency situations, providing a quick and reliable means of communication in case of an emergency.

However, there are also some serious drawbacks to consider. For example, exposure to cell phone radiation has been linked to headaches, sleep problems, and even cancer. Furthermore, the constant distraction of cell phones has been shown to affect our ability to focus and concentrate, leading to decreased productivity and a decline in cognitive abilities. Additionally, the increased use of cell phones has been linked to feelings of isolation and a decline in face-to-face communication skills. As a result, some argue that cell phones have had a negative impact on our social interactions and relationships.

To wrap things up, while cell phones have certainly brought many benefits to our lives, it is also important to consider the negative impacts they have had on our health and social interactions. While it may not be possible to completely eliminate these negative effects, it is important that we use cell phones in a responsible and balanced way. This may involve setting limits on screen time, investing in research to better understand the impact of cell phone radiation, and encouraging face-to-face communication and social interaction. Ultimately, by being mindful of the impact of cell phones on our lives, we can ensure that they continue to be a positive force for good.

Social Media

The rise of social media has had a profound impact on our society and the way we interact with each other. While some argue that social media has greatly improved our lives by providing new opportunities for communication and self-expression, others believe that it has had negative consequences for our mental health and social relationships. In this essay, I will explore both the positive and negative aspects of social media and come to a conclusion about its overall impact.

On the positive side, social media has created new avenues for communication and self-expression. For example, platforms such as Facebook and Instagram allow us to easily connect with friends and family members, share our experiences and thoughts with a wider audience, and form new connections with people from all over the world. Additionally, social media has been a powerful tool for activism and social change, allowing individuals and organizations to spread their message and mobilize support.

However, there are also many negative consequences to consider. For example, the constant comparison to others on social media can lead to feelings of inadequacy and low self-esteem. Additionally, excessive use of social media has been linked to depression, anxiety, and other mental health problems. Furthermore, social media can also be a source of negativity and cyberbullying, leading to feelings of fear and insecurity.

To conclude, while social media has certainly brought many benefits to our lives, it is also important to consider the negative impacts it has had on our mental health and social relationships. While it may not be possible to completely eliminate these negative effects, it is important that we use social media in a responsible and mindful way. This may involve setting limits on screen time, actively seeking out positive and uplifting content, and being mindful of the impact that our online behaviour can have on others. By doing so, we can ensure that social media continues to be a positive force for good in our lives.

Genetically Modified Crops

The issue of genetically modified crops has been a controversial topic for many years. Some believe that genetically modifying crops is necessary to feed the growing global population and provide food security, while others argue that it is dangerous and could have long-term consequences for both the environment and human health. In this essay, I will examine both sides of the argument and come to a conclusion about the use of genetically modified crops.

On the one hand, proponents of genetically modified crops argue that they are necessary to address the growing food security crisis. With the global population expected to reach 9.7 billion by 2050, they argue that we need to find new ways to increase crop yields and make food production more efficient. By genetically modifying crops, scientists can create new strains that are more resistant to pests, diseases, and environmental conditions, leading to higher crop yields and more food for a growing population.

However, there are also many concerns about the potential dangers of genetically modified crops. For example, some worry that they could lead to the creation of "superweeds" that are resistant to herbicides and difficult to control. Additionally, there are concerns about the impact that genetically modified crops could have on the environment, including the potential for gene flow between crops and wild relatives, which could lead to the spread of unwanted traits. Furthermore, there are concerns about the impact that genetically modified crops could have on human health, including the potential for allergenicity, toxicity, and long-term health effects.

In conclusion, the issue of genetically modified crops is a complex and multifaceted one, and it is important to consider both the potential benefits and drawbacks of this technology. While it may be tempting to believe that genetically modified crops are the solution to our food security crisis, it is also important to carefully consider the potential dangers and long-term consequences of this technology. By doing so, we can ensure that genetically modified crops are used in a responsible and sustainable way, to the benefit of both the environment and human health.

Globalization: Boon or Bane?

Globalization refers to the increasing interconnectedness and interdependence of the world's economies, societies, and cultures. While some argue that globalization has brought numerous benefits, including economic growth, increased trade, and greater cultural exchange, others believe that it has had negative consequences, including job loss, cultural homogenization, and income inequality. In this essay, I will examine both the positive and negative aspects of globalization and come to a conclusion about its overall impact.

On the positive side, globalization has had a profound impact on the global economy, leading to increased trade, investment, and economic growth. This has led to the creation of new jobs and improved living standards for people around the world. Additionally, globalization has facilitated the exchange of ideas, cultures, and technology, leading to a greater understanding and appreciation of different cultures and ways of life.

However, there are also many negative consequences to consider. For example, globalization has led to the loss of jobs in some countries as companies move production to countries with lower labour costs. Additionally, globalization has led to increased income inequality, as the benefits of economic growth are not evenly distributed. Furthermore, there are concerns that globalization is leading to cultural homogenization, as people around the world become increasingly alike and traditional cultures are lost.

All in all, while globalization has certainly brought many benefits to our world, it is also important to consider the negative consequences that it has had. While it may not be possible to completely eliminate these negative effects, it is important that we work to mitigate them and ensure that the benefits of globalization are more evenly distributed. This may involve supporting policies that promote fair trade, protecting workers' rights, and investing in education and training programs to help people adapt to the changing global economy. By doing so, we can ensure that globalization continues to be a positive force for good in our world.

Impact of Social Media on Relationships

Social media has become a ubiquitous part of our lives, with billions of people around the world using platforms like Facebook, Instagram, and Twitter to connect with friends and family, share content, and express their thoughts and feelings. However, the impact of social media on relationships has been a subject of much debate in recent years. Some argue that social media has made it easier for people to connect and maintain relationships, while others believe that it has had a negative impact on relationships by fostering comparison and competition, promoting superficiality, and eroding privacy.

One argument in favour of social media is that it has made it easier for people to stay in touch and maintain relationships, regardless of distance and time. With the ability to instantaneously message, video chat, and share updates, social media has allowed people to remain connected even when they are physically separated. For example, individuals can use social media to stay connected with friends and family members who live far away, to keep up with the lives of people they care about, and to build and maintain new relationships.

However, there are also many negative aspects of social media that can impact relationships. For one, social media can foster comparison and competition, as people are constantly exposed to highly curated images and updates from friends and acquaintances. This can lead to feelings of inadequacy and insecurity, and can even erode self-esteem over time. Additionally, social media often promotes superficiality, as people feel pressure to present a highly curated and idealized version of themselves online. This can result in a lack of authenticity in relationships, as people struggle to reconcile their online and offline identities.

Furthermore, social media has also been criticized for eroding privacy and violating trust in relationships. With the ability to easily share personal information and updates, individuals may feel that their privacy has been violated, as they are bombarded with personal details about friends and acquaintances. Moreover, social media has been linked to infidelity, as people are increasingly using platforms like Tinder and other dating apps to meet and interact with potential partners. This can lead to a breakdown of trust in relationships, as people struggle to balance their online and offline identities.

To conclude, the impact of social media on relationships is a complex and multifaceted issue that requires careful consideration. While it is true that social media has made it easier for people to stay in touch and maintain relationships, it has also had many negative impacts, including fostering comparison and competition, promoting superficiality, and eroding privacy and trust. Ultimately, the impact of social media on relationships will depend on how individuals use it and the choices they make in how they interact with others online.

Nature or Nurture?

The nature vs. nurture debate has been ongoing for centuries, and is centred around the question of whether intelligence is primarily determined by genetics (nature) or by environmental factors and experiences (nurture). Those who believe that intelligence is largely determined by genetics argue that our genes influence our cognitive abilities, such as memory, problem-solving skills, and language. On the other hand, those who believe that intelligence is primarily shaped by environmental factors point to evidence that early childhood experiences, such as educational opportunities, can have a significant impact on cognitive development.

One argument in favour of nature is that numerous studies have found a genetic component to intelligence. For example, twin studies have shown that intelligence is highly heritable, with identical twins being more similar in intelligence than fraternal twins. Additionally, genetic research has identified specific genes that are associated with intelligence, such as the DRD2 gene. These findings suggest that genetics play a role in determining intelligence.

However, the argument for nurture is also compelling. Evidence shows that early childhood experiences can have a significant impact on cognitive development. For example, studies have found that children who grow up in poverty or experience neglect or abuse are more likely to struggle with cognitive development and have lower IQ scores. Additionally, early childhood education has been shown to have a positive impact on intelligence, with children who receive high-quality early education performing better on cognitive tests later in life.

It is also important to consider the interaction between nature and nurture. For example, genetics may determine a person's baseline level of intelligence, but environmental factors can still have a significant impact on their cognitive abilities. For instance, a child with a high genetic potential for intelligence may still struggle with cognitive development if they do not receive adequate educational opportunities.

The bottom line is this. The nature vs. nurture debate is complex and multi-faceted. While both genetics and environmental factors play a role in determining intelligence, it is likely that the relationship is more complex than a simple nature or nurture dichotomy. The most likely explanation is that intelligence is influenced by a combination of genetic and environmental factors, with each having a unique impact on cognitive development. By considering both nature and nurture, we can gain a more complete understanding of the complex and dynamic factors that influence intelligence.

The Moderation Paradox: Debating the Merits of Pursuing Financial Stability over Extreme Wealth

In today's society, many people are driven by the desire to become wealthy, with the belief that wealth brings happiness and success. On the other hand, others argue that moderation is the key to a happy and fulfilling life, and that excessive wealth can actually lead to negative outcomes. In this essay, I will argue that while the pursuit of wealth can be tempting, it is often better to aim for financial stability and moderation rather than extreme wealth.

One argument in favour of staying moderate is that excessive wealth can lead to negative outcomes, such as stress, anxiety, and dissatisfaction. Research has shown that once people's basic needs are met, additional wealth does not bring a significant increase in happiness. In fact, for some, the pursuit of wealth can lead to increased stress and anxiety, as they are constantly worried about maintaining their wealth and financial stability.

Another argument in favour of moderation is that it is more sustainable in the long term. While getting rich quickly may seem attractive, it is often achieved through unsustainable methods, such as gambling or high-risk investments. In contrast, moderate financial stability is more likely to be achieved through steady and consistent work and saving. This can provide a more secure and stable foundation for a happy and fulfilling life.

Additionally, staying moderate allows us to focus on other aspects of life that are important for our well-being, such as relationships, health, and personal growth. When we are not constantly chasing wealth, we can devote more time and energy to these important areas of our lives, which can lead to greater happiness and fulfilment.

It is also worth considering the impact of wealth on others and the world around us. The pursuit of wealth can often lead to a focus on material possessions and a disregard for the needs of others. In contrast, moderation and financial stability can provide us with the means to help others and make a positive impact on the world.

To summarize, while the pursuit of wealth may seem tempting, it is often better to aim for financial stability and moderation. Excessive wealth can lead to negative outcomes, such as stress and anxiety, and is often unsustainable in the long term. By focusing on moderation, we can achieve a more balanced and fulfilling life, while also making a positive impact on the world around us.

The Use of Smartphones in Schools

The use of smartphones in schools has become a controversial topic, with many people having differing opinions on whether or not students should be allowed to bring their smartphones to school. In this essay, I will present arguments for and against allowing students to bring smartphones to school.

One argument in favour of allowing students to bring smartphones to school is that they can be used as a learning tool. Smartphones are equipped with a variety of educational apps and resources that can be used to support learning. For example, students can use their smartphones to access online textbooks, educational videos, and interactive quizzes. In addition, students can use their smartphones to communicate with their teachers and classmates, which can help to promote collaboration and teamwork.

Another argument in favour of allowing students to bring smartphones to school is that they can be used for safety purposes. In case of an emergency, students can use their smartphones to call for help or to contact their parents. Additionally, students can use their smartphones to access important information, such as school schedules and policies, in real-time.

However, there are also arguments against allowing students to bring smartphones to school. One argument is that smartphones can be a distraction during class. Students may be tempted to use their smartphones for non-academic purposes, such as playing games or browsing social media, which can take away from their learning and attention in class. Furthermore, students may be exposed to inappropriate or harmful content on their smartphones, which can have a negative impact on their well-being.

Another argument against allowing students to bring smartphones to school is that they can be used for cheating. Students may be able to access answers to tests or assignments on their smartphones, which can compromise the integrity of the educational process. In addition, smartphones can be used to share answers or cheat in group assignments, which can undermine the learning experience for everyone involved.

On the whole, the debate over whether students should be allowed to bring smartphones to school is complex and multifaceted. While there are arguments in favour of allowing students to bring smartphones to school, such as their potential to support learning and enhance safety, there are also arguments against allowing them, such as the potential for distraction and cheating. Ultimately, the decision on whether or not students should be allowed to bring smartphones to school should be based on a careful consideration of the potential benefits and drawbacks, and may vary from school to school based on the needs and priorities of the students and community.

The Use of Robots in the Workforce

Robots have been a part of the workforce for decades, but in recent years, advances in technology have made robots increasingly capable of performing a wide range of tasks that were once the exclusive domain of human workers. While the use of robots in the workforce has many benefits, including increased efficiency, accuracy, and cost savings, it has also raised some important ethical and social questions.

On one hand, the use of robots in the workforce can help to increase productivity and efficiency. By automating repetitive and time-consuming tasks, robots can free up human workers to focus on more complex and creative work, improving overall performance and reducing the risk of errors. Furthermore, robots are often able to work longer hours and at a faster pace than human workers, which can help to increase output and reduce costs.

However, the widespread use of robots in the workforce also raises important ethical and social concerns. One of the main concerns is the potential for widespread job displacement, as robots take over many of the jobs that were once performed by human workers. This can lead to increased unemployment and poverty, as people struggle to find work and support themselves. Additionally, robots may also create a sense of inequality and social stratification, as highly-skilled workers who are able to operate and maintain robots are more likely to be in demand, while less-skilled workers are left behind.

Furthermore, the use of robots in the workforce can also raise questions about accountability and liability. If a robot causes harm or makes a mistake, it can be difficult to determine who is responsible and who should be held accountable. This can lead to a lack of accountability and a breakdown of trust in the workforce, as people struggle to navigate this new and complex landscape.

All in all, while the use of robots in the workforce has many benefits, it also raises important ethical and social concerns. As robots become increasingly prevalent in the workforce, it is essential that policymakers, businesses, and workers work together to ensure that the benefits of automation are shared fairly and that the risks are minimized. This may include supporting retraining programs for workers who are displaced by robots, establishing clear rules and regulations around the use of robots in the workforce, and creating systems of accountability and liability to ensure that robots are used responsibly and ethically.

The Use of Genetically Modified Organisms (GMOs) in Agriculture

The use of genetically modified organisms (GMOs) in agriculture has been a controversial issue for many years, with arguments for and against their use. On one hand, proponents of GMOs argue that they can help to increase yields, reduce the use of pesticides, and improve the overall quality and nutritional value of crops. On the other hand, critics argue that GMOs are a threat to biodiversity and can have negative impacts on human health and the environment.

One of the main arguments in favour of GMOs is that they can help to increase yields and reduce the use of pesticides. By engineering crops to be more resistant to pests and diseases, farmers can reduce the amount of pesticides they need to use, which can be both costly and harmful to the environment. Additionally, GMOs can be designed to be more productive, yielding higher quantities of crops with improved nutritional quality.

However, opponents of GMOs argue that they are a threat to biodiversity, as they can have negative impacts on other plants and animals in the ecosystem. By creating crops that are resistant to pests and diseases, GMOs can also create new pests and diseases, as pests and diseases that were once controlled by traditional methods are now able to evolve and overcome the new resistance. Additionally, GMOs can also crossbreed with wild relatives, creating hybrid organisms that can spread and displace native species.

Another concern about GMOs is their potential impact on human health. Some critics argue that GMOs can contain allergens or toxins that are harmful to humans and that there is not enough research to determine their long-term safety. Additionally, there is a concern that GMOs could create unintended health consequences, such as the development of antibiotic-resistant bacteria or the creation of new allergens.

To wrap things up, while the use of GMOs in agriculture has many potential benefits, it also raises important concerns about biodiversity and human health. As the use of GMOs continues to grow, it is essential that policymakers and scientists work together to ensure that their use is safe and responsible. This may include conducting more research to determine their long-term safety, establishing clear regulations around their use, and monitoring their impacts on the environment and human health over time.

The Benefits and Drawbacks of Public Transportation

Public transportation is an important aspect of modern cities, providing an alternative to driving and offering a convenient and cost-effective way to get around. While there are many benefits to using public transportation, there are also some drawbacks that must be considered.

One of the main benefits of public transportation is that it can reduce traffic congestion and air pollution. By providing an alternative to driving, public transportation can help to reduce the number of cars on the road, which can reduce traffic congestion, improve air quality, and reduce greenhouse gas emissions. Additionally, public transportation is often more energy-efficient than driving, as it can transport many people using one vehicle, which reduces the amount of energy used per person.

Another benefit of public transportation is that it can be a more cost-effective option for many people, especially those who do not have access to a car or who live in areas with high costs of living. Public transportation is often cheaper than driving, and it can also save people money on things like gas, insurance, and maintenance. Additionally, public transportation can provide greater access to jobs and other opportunities, as it can reach areas that are not served by cars or that are difficult to reach by car.

However, there are also some drawbacks to public transportation that must be considered. One of the main drawbacks is that it can be less convenient than driving, especially for people who live in areas with limited public transportation options. Additionally, public transportation can be less reliable than driving, as it is subject to delays, cancellations, and other disruptions. Additionally, public transportation can be less flexible than driving, as it may not go exactly where you want to go, and it may not be available at the time you want to travel.

Another drawback of public transportation is that it can be less comfortable than driving, especially for people who are used to the privacy and comfort of their own car. Public transportation can be crowded, noisy, and uncomfortable, which can be especially challenging for people with disabilities or for those who are traveling with children or large items.

At the end of the day, while public transportation has many benefits, it also has some drawbacks that must be considered. To maximize the benefits of public transportation, it is essential that policymakers invest in improving public transportation systems, including expanding routes, increasing frequency and reliability, and improving the comfort and accessibility of public transportation vehicles. Additionally, people who choose to use public transportation must be prepared to make some compromises in terms of convenience and comfort, but with the right investment and support, public transportation can play an important role in creating more sustainable and liveable cities for all.

The Benefits and Drawbacks of Advertising

Advertising is an essential aspect of modern commerce, playing a critical role in promoting products and services, creating demand, and driving economic growth. While there are many benefits to advertising, there are also some drawbacks that must be considered.

One of the main benefits of advertising is that it provides valuable information to consumers, helping them to make informed decisions about the products and services they purchase. By highlighting the features and benefits of different products and services, advertising can help consumers to compare and choose the best options for their needs. Additionally, advertising can help to stimulate economic growth by creating demand for new and existing products and services, which can drive innovation and create jobs.

Another benefit of advertising is that it supports freedom of speech and the press, allowing people to express their opinions and ideas freely and openly. Advertising can be an important tool for promoting public awareness and advocacy, as it provides a platform for voices that might otherwise go unheard. Additionally, advertising can support the growth of new and emerging businesses, as it provides a way for start-ups and entrepreneurs to reach new customers and build their brand.

However, there are also some drawbacks to advertising that must be considered. One of the main drawbacks is that it can be misleading or inaccurate, leading consumers to make poor decisions based on false or incomplete information. Additionally, advertising can be intrusive, as it often uses tactics like pop-up ads, banners, and pre-roll videos to reach consumers, which can be annoying and distracting.

Another drawback of advertising is that it can contribute to the proliferation of consumerism and materialism, leading people to focus on acquiring more and more material goods, even when they do not need them. Additionally, advertising can be harmful to public health, as it often promotes unhealthy products like junk food and tobacco, which can contribute to chronic diseases like obesity, heart disease, and cancer.

To summarize, while advertising has many benefits, it also has some drawbacks that must be considered. To maximize the benefits of advertising and minimize the drawbacks, it is essential that policymakers and industry leaders take steps to regulate advertising practices, to ensure that advertising is truthful, accurate, and does not harm public health or contribute to negative social trends. Additionally, consumers must be vigilant and critical in their evaluations of advertising messages, taking the time to understand what is being advertised and the implications of their purchases. With the right regulation and consumer engagement, advertising can play a positive role in promoting economic growth and supporting public awareness, while also fostering sustainable and responsible consumer behaviour.

The Role of Technology in Education

The integration of technology in education has been a topic of great discussion in recent years. On one hand, technology has the potential to revolutionize the way we teach and learn, making education more accessible, interactive and personalized. On the other hand, some argue that excessive dependence on technology in the classroom can detract from the human element of education and negatively affect students' critical thinking and problem-solving skills.

Advocates of technology in education argue that it has the potential to enhance students' learning experiences by making it more engaging and interactive. For example, educational software and online resources can help students visualize complex concepts and make them easier to understand. Additionally, technology can provide students with access to a wealth of information and resources that would otherwise be unavailable.

However, critics argue that the over-reliance on technology in the classroom can have negative effects on students' cognitive development. They claim that technology can reduce the need for critical thinking and problem-solving skills as students become too reliant on screens to provide answers. Furthermore, they argue that technology can lead to a lack of human interaction and a decrease in face-to-face communication skills, which are essential for building healthy relationships and successful careers.

Another concern is that technology in education may exacerbate socio-economic inequalities. While students from affluent families may have access to the latest technology and educational resources, those from lower-income families may not. This can result in a digital divide that only widens the gap between the haves and have-nots.

To conclude, while technology has the potential to transform education for the better, it is important to approach its integration in the classroom with caution. The benefits of technology must be balanced against its potential negative effects on students' cognitive development and socio-economic inequalities. Ultimately, the goal should be to find a way to harness technology's potential to enhance the educational experience while also maintaining a human touch.

Alternative Medicine: A Viable Option or a Risky Experiment?

In recent years, alternative forms of medicine, such as herbal remedies, acupuncture, and chiropractic, have gained popularity as more people seek out natural and holistic ways to treat their illnesses and maintain their health. While some view alternative medicine as a viable option, others see it as a risky experiment with little scientific basis. In this essay, I will argue that while alternative medicine may have its benefits, it is important to approach it with caution and consider the potential risks.

One argument in favour of alternative medicine is that it can be more natural and holistic than traditional medicine, which often relies on synthetic drugs and surgery. Alternative medicine can help to address the root cause of a condition, rather than simply treating its symptoms, and can also help to promote overall health and well-being.

However, there are also several risks associated with alternative medicine. One of the biggest concerns is that many alternative treatments have not been thoroughly studied or scientifically tested, and therefore their effectiveness and safety are uncertain. In addition, some alternative remedies can interact with traditional medications and have harmful side effects, making it important to consult with a doctor before trying them.

Another concern with alternative medicine is that it can sometimes be used to avoid seeking necessary medical treatment, which can lead to serious health consequences. For example, a person who relies on herbal remedies to treat a serious condition like cancer may be putting their health at risk by not seeking appropriate medical care.

It is also important to consider the quality and regulation of alternative medicines. Many alternative remedies are not regulated by the government, meaning that there is no way to ensure that they are safe or effective. This can lead to the use of counterfeit or low-quality products, which can be dangerous and ineffective.

All in all, while alternative medicine may offer some benefits, it is important to approach it with caution and consider the potential risks. It is always advisable to seek professional medical advice before trying any new form of treatment, and to make informed decisions based on the available evidence. Alternative medicine can be a useful complement to traditional medicine, but it is important to understand its limitations and be mindful of the potential dangers.

Balancing Progress and Preservation: The Debate over Demolishing Historical Buildings for High-Rise Development

The world is constantly evolving and developing, and cities are no exception. With the increasing population and demand for housing, many cities are turning to high-rise buildings as a solution. However, this often involves the demolition of historical buildings, which raises the question of whether it is worth sacrificing the past for the sake of progress. On one hand, proponents of high-rise development argue that it is necessary for accommodating a growing population and meeting the needs of modern society. On the other hand, opponents argue that preserving historical buildings is important for maintaining the cultural heritage of a city. In this essay, I will argue that while progress is important, it should be balanced with the preservation of historical buildings.

One argument in favour of preserving historical buildings is their cultural and historical significance. These buildings are a representation of the city's history and its unique identity, and they offer a glimpse into the past. By demolishing these buildings, we risk losing a part of our cultural heritage and history, which can never be regained. In addition, historical buildings can also serve as tourist attractions, which can generate significant revenue for the city.

Another argument in favour of preserving historical buildings is their architectural value. These buildings are often designed with intricate details and a unique aesthetic, which are a reflection of the art and architecture of their time. Demolishing these buildings can also result in the loss of important works of architecture, which would be a significant blow to the field.

However, proponents of high-rise development argue that it is necessary for accommodating a growing population and meeting the needs of modern society. High-rise buildings can provide more housing options, which can help alleviate the housing crisis in many cities. In addition, high-rise buildings can also provide modern amenities and facilities that are essential for contemporary living.

In a nutshell, while the development of high-rise buildings is necessary for meeting the needs of a growing population, it should be balanced with the preservation of historical buildings. Historical buildings are important for maintaining the cultural heritage and identity of a city, and they provide a unique architectural and historical value that cannot be replaced. By striking a balance between progress and preservation, cities can continue to grow and develop while still maintaining their unique character and history.

Should the Elderly be Sent to Old Folks Homes?

As people grow older, they often face a number of challenges that can make it difficult for them to live independently. Some families choose to send their elderly loved ones to old folks' homes, believing that this is the best way to ensure that they receive the care and support they need. However, this decision is often met with opposition, as some people argue that sending the elderly to these homes is cruel and fails to take into account their emotional needs. In this essay, I will argue that while old folks' homes can provide a valuable service for some elderly individuals, they should not be considered the only option for those who need care and support.

One argument in favour of old folks' homes is that they provide a level of professional care that is difficult to match in a family setting. Staff at these homes are trained to meet the unique needs of elderly individuals, including managing medical conditions, providing physical support, and addressing emotional needs. In many cases, this level of care is necessary to ensure that the elderly receive the best possible quality of life.

However, it is also worth considering the impact that old folks' homes can have on the emotional well-being of elderly individuals. For many elderly people, these homes can feel like a prison, with strict schedules, limited social interactions, and a lack of personal space. This can lead to feelings of loneliness, depression, and a loss of independence, which can have a significant impact on their quality of life.

Additionally, it is important to consider the cost of old folks' homes, as they can be expensive, especially for those who need long-term care. This can be a significant burden for families, who may struggle to find the funds to pay for this care. Furthermore, the cost of care at these homes can rise over time, making it difficult for families to keep up with the payments.

A better solution for many elderly individuals might be to provide in-home care, which can allow them to continue living in the comfort of their own homes. This can be a more cost-effective option, and it can also provide elderly individuals with the support they need, while also allowing them to maintain a degree of independence and control over their lives.

To summarize, while old folks' homes can provide a valuable service for some elderly individuals, they should not be considered the only option for those who need care and support. The emotional impact of living in these homes, combined with the cost, make it important to consider alternative options, such as in-home care, to ensure that the elderly receive the best possible quality of life.

Technology and its Impact on Human Laziness: A Controversial Debate

In recent years, technology has rapidly advanced and infiltrated every aspect of our lives, making many tasks easier and more convenient. However, this convenience has led to a growing concern about the impact of technology on human laziness. On one hand, proponents argue that technology has made our lives easier, allowing us to spend more time relaxing and enjoying our leisure time. On the other hand, critics argue that technology has made us increasingly lazy and dependent on machines to do even the simplest tasks for us.

One argument in favour of technology is that it has made many tasks quicker and more efficient. For example, we can now complete shopping, banking, and other daily tasks from the comfort of our own homes using a computer or mobile device. This has freed up more time for people to relax and engage in other activities that they enjoy. Furthermore, technology has also made it easier for people to stay connected with friends and family, regardless of their location, which has increased overall happiness and well-being.

However, there is also a valid argument against technology, which is that it is making us increasingly lazy. With the rise of automation and AI, many tasks that used to require manual labour can now be done by machines. This has led to a decrease in physical activity and an increase in sedentary lifestyles, which can lead to a range of health problems such as obesity, heart disease, and diabetes. Furthermore, the constant distraction and stimulation from screens and technology can also reduce our ability to focus and concentrate, making it more difficult for us to complete tasks that require sustained attention.

Another argument against technology is that it is making us more dependent on machines to complete even the simplest tasks for us. For example, we now have devices that can perform tasks like vacuuming, washing dishes, and even preparing food for us. This has made it easier for people to avoid physical activity and become less self-sufficient. In turn, this can lead to decreased creativity, critical thinking skills, and a decline in manual dexterity.

At the end of the day, technology has both positive and negative impacts on human laziness. While it has made many tasks quicker and more efficient, it has also made us increasingly dependent on machines to complete even the simplest tasks for us. To ensure that technology does not have a negative impact on our physical and mental well-being, it is important to use it in moderation and to engage in physical activity and other forms of leisure that promote a healthy and balanced lifestyle.

The Ethics of Animal Testing: Balancing Scientific Advancements with Animal Welfare

Animal testing has been a controversial topic for decades, with strong arguments on both sides. On one hand, proponents argue that animal testing is necessary for scientific advancements and the development of new treatments and medicines. On the other hand, opponents argue that animal testing is cruel and inhumane, and that there are alternative methods that can provide similar results without causing harm to animals. In this essay, I will argue that while animal testing may provide valuable scientific insights, it should be regulated and limited to ensure that animal welfare is protected.

One argument in favour of animal testing is that it has led to significant scientific advancements and the development of new treatments and medicines. For example, animal testing has played a crucial role in the development of life-saving drugs and treatments for a range of diseases, including cancer, heart disease, and HIV/AIDS. Proponents argue that animal testing is essential for the continued progress of medical science and the advancement of human health.

However, despite its scientific benefits, animal testing raises serious ethical concerns. Animal welfare groups argue that testing is cruel and inhumane, and that animals are subjected to significant pain and suffering. Furthermore, animal testing is not always accurate or reliable, as results from animal studies may not accurately reflect how a treatment will affect humans.

To balance the scientific benefits of animal testing with the need to protect animal welfare, it is crucial that animal testing be regulated and limited. This could include the use of alternative methods, such as computer simulations, tissue cultures, and microdosing studies, which can provide similar results without causing harm to animals. Additionally, regulations should be put in place to ensure that animal testing is conducted in a humane and ethical manner, with strict protocols in place to minimize pain and suffering.

In short, while animal testing may provide valuable scientific insights, it should be limited and regulated to ensure that animal welfare is protected. Alternatives should be explored and utilized, and regulations should be put in place to ensure that animal testing is conducted in a humane and ethical manner. By balancing the scientific benefits of animal testing with the need to protect animal welfare, we can ensure that advances in medical science are achieved in an ethical and responsible manner.

Plastic or Paper: Which is the Better Option for the Environment?

In recent years, the issue of waste management has become a major concern for many people, as the amount of waste generated by human activities continues to grow. One of the most important debates in the waste management industry is whether plastic or paper is the better option for the environment. While both materials have their pros and cons, it is clear that plastic is the more harmful option and that we should do all we can to reduce our use of it.

One of the main arguments in favour of paper is that it is biodegradable, meaning that it will naturally break down over time and become part of the environment. In contrast, plastic is not biodegradable and can take hundreds of years to break down. This means that plastic waste will persist in the environment for a very long time, causing harm to wildlife and ecosystems and contributing to the growing problem of plastic pollution.

Another argument in favour of paper is that it is more sustainable. The production of paper requires less energy and generates fewer greenhouse gas emissions than the production of plastic. Furthermore, paper is often made from sustainable resources, such as recycled paper or sustainably managed forests. In contrast, plastic is typically made from fossil fuels, which are finite resources that contribute to climate change when burned for energy.

Despite the advantages of paper over plastic, it is important to note that paper has its own environmental downsides. For example, paper production often involves the use of harmful chemicals and the deforestation of important habitats. Additionally, paper must be transported to consumers, which contributes to air and water pollution.

In conclusion, while both plastic and paper have their environmental drawbacks, it is clear that plastic is the more harmful option. To reduce the impact of waste on the environment, we should do all we can to reduce our use of plastic and shift to more sustainable alternatives, such as paper. By making this change, we can help to protect the environment and preserve it for future generations.

Plastic Versus Paper Waste

The debate surrounding the use of plastic versus paper waste has been ongoing for many years, with individuals holding strong opinions on both sides of the argument. Some argue that plastic is the more convenient and cost-effective option, while others believe that paper waste is a more environmentally friendly choice.

One argument in favour of plastic waste is that it is more durable and can be used multiple times, reducing the need for continuous production and disposal of new materials. Plastic is also lightweight, making it easier to transport and reducing the carbon footprint of transportation. In addition, plastic can be easily recycled and transformed into new products, helping to reduce waste and conserve natural resources.

On the other hand, proponents of paper waste argue that it is a more environmentally friendly option, as it is biodegradable and does not contribute to the build-up of non-biodegradable waste in landfills. Paper products are also made from renewable resources, such as trees, which can be replanted and regenerated, whereas plastic is made from finite petroleum resources. Furthermore, the production of paper products requires less energy and produces fewer greenhouse gas emissions compared to the production of plastic.

Another argument in favour of paper waste is that it is a more sustainable option, as it can be composted and used as a natural fertilizer, while plastic can take hundreds of years to decompose. In addition, paper products are often made from recycled materials, reducing the need for virgin materials and further conserving natural resources.

However, it is important to consider the potential negative impact of paper waste on the environment. The production of paper products requires large amounts of water, energy, and chemicals, leading to increased greenhouse gas emissions and pollution. In addition, the transportation of paper products can result in a significant carbon footprint, as paper is heavier than plastic and requires more energy to transport.

To wrap things up, the debate surrounding the use of plastic versus paper waste is complex and multifaceted, with strong arguments on both sides. While plastic has certain advantages, such as durability and ease of recycling, it is important to consider the environmental impact of plastic production and disposal. On the other hand, while paper waste is biodegradable and made from renewable resources, it also has its own environmental consequences, such as the production of greenhouse gases and the use of large amounts of water and energy. Ultimately, the decision between plastic and paper waste should be based on a balanced consideration of the potential benefits and drawbacks of each option.

Preventing Crime: Is There More That Can Be Done or Is It Beyond Our Control?

In today's society, crime is a constant concern for many individuals and communities. Some argue that there is much that can be done to prevent crime and that it is simply a matter of implementing the right strategies and solutions. Others, however, believe that preventing crime is beyond our control and that no matter what we do, crime will always be a part of society.

On one hand, those who believe that there is more that can be done to prevent crime argue that the root causes of crime, such as poverty, lack of education, and mental health issues, must be addressed. By addressing these underlying factors, it is possible to reduce the number of individuals who are at risk of committing crimes and to create safer communities. Additionally, implementing effective crime prevention strategies, such as community policing and neighbourhood watch programs, can also help to reduce the incidence of crime.

However, those who believe that preventing crime is beyond our control argue that there will always be individuals who engage in criminal activities, no matter what preventative measures are put in place. They believe that it is impossible to completely eliminate crime and that we must accept that crime will always be a part of society.

Another perspective is that while it may not be possible to completely eliminate crime, there is still much that can be done to reduce its occurrence and impact. This might include investing in education and employment programs, addressing mental health issues, and providing support for at-risk individuals. By doing so, it is possible to reduce the number of individuals who are likely to engage in criminal activities and to create safer communities.

Additionally, it is important to acknowledge the role of the criminal justice system in preventing crime. This can include the use of rehabilitation programs, alternative forms of punishment, and efforts to address systemic issues such as racial discrimination and mass incarceration. By improving the criminal justice system and addressing the root causes of crime, it is possible to reduce the incidence of crime and create a safer society.

In conclusion, the debate over whether there is more that can be done to prevent crime or if it is beyond our control is ongoing. While it may not be possible to completely eliminate crime, there is still much that can be done to reduce its occurrence and impact. By addressing the root causes of crime and implementing effective prevention strategies, it is possible to create safer communities and a more just society.

The Debate on Whether Hitting the Gym or Staying at Home Exercise is More Effective for Achieving Fitness Goals

The topic of exercise has been a source of much debate and discussion over the years, with some people advocating for hitting the gym and others promoting the benefits of staying at home exercises. While both methods have their advantages, there is a growing body of evidence that suggests that hitting the gym may be more effective in achieving fitness goals.

One of the main advantages of hitting the gym is that it provides access to a wide range of equipment and facilities, allowing individuals to engage in a variety of different exercises and routines. This can be particularly beneficial for those who are looking to build muscle mass or improve their overall fitness levels. Additionally, hitting the gym can be a great way to socialize and meet like-minded people, which can be an important factor in staying motivated and committed to fitness goals.

However, there are also some disadvantages to hitting the gym, including the cost of membership and the time required to travel to and from the gym. This can make it difficult for some people to stick to a consistent exercise routine, particularly those who are busy or have limited financial resources. Additionally, the busy and noisy environment of a gym can be distracting for some people, making it difficult to focus on their exercises and reach their goals.

Staying at home exercise, on the other hand, provides a number of advantages, including convenience and cost-effectiveness. It is much easier to fit into a busy schedule, and can be done without the need for expensive equipment or memberships. Additionally, exercising at home can be a great way to get some fresh air and natural light, which can help to boost energy levels and improve overall health.

However, there are also some drawbacks to staying at home exercise. For example, it can be difficult to maintain motivation without the structure and social support provided by hitting the gym. Additionally, individuals may struggle to create effective and challenging workout routines without access to professional guidance and specialized equipment.

In a nutshell, the debate over whether hitting the gym or staying at home exercise is more effective for achieving fitness goals is a complex and multifaceted issue. While both methods have their advantages and disadvantages, the best approach will depend on individual circumstances, goals, and preferences. Ultimately, the most important thing is to find a method of exercise that is sustainable, enjoyable, and effective in helping individuals reach their fitness goals.

Moving Out or Staying Put: The Age-Old Debate on Living with Parents at 30

In today's society, there is a growing trend among young adults to live with their parents well into their thirties. While some view this as a necessary step to save money and build a solid financial foundation, others believe that it is time to move out and become independent by the age of 30. In this essay, I will argue that whether to move out or stay with parents is a personal decision that depends on individual circumstances, but that there are benefits and drawbacks to both options.

One argument in favour of moving out is that it provides an opportunity to build independence and take responsibility for one's life. Living on one's own requires self-sufficiency, including budgeting, meal planning, and household chores. This can help young adults develop essential life skills and gain a sense of pride and self-worth.

Another argument for moving out is that it can provide a sense of privacy and personal space. Living with parents, even well into adulthood, can be challenging for some individuals who feel that their privacy and freedom are limited. Moving out can provide an escape from these constraints and a chance to create one's own lifestyle.

However, there are also compelling arguments for staying with parents. One advantage is the financial savings. Rent, utilities, and other living expenses can be substantial, and by staying with parents, young adults can save money and reduce their financial burden. This can provide a solid foundation for their future and allow them to focus on other important goals, such as paying off debt, building an emergency fund, or saving for a down payment on a house.

Another advantage of staying with parents is the emotional support and comfort of familiar surroundings. Living with family can provide a sense of security and comfort that can be difficult to find elsewhere. This can be especially important for those who are struggling with mental health issues, who have recently experienced a loss, or who are facing other challenges in life.

To conclude, the decision of whether to move out or stay with parents by the age of 30 is a personal one that depends on individual circumstances and priorities. Both options have their benefits and drawbacks, but ultimately, it is up to each young adult to weigh the pros and cons and make the decision that is right for them. Whether it's for financial stability, personal growth, or emotional support, it's important to choose a living situation that supports one's well-being and overall happiness.

House or Car: Which Should You Invest in First?

In today's society, buying a house and a car are two of the most common goals for people when it comes to achieving financial stability and independence. However, there is often a debate about which one should come first - a house or a car. Some argue that it is more practical and financially sound to buy a house first, while others argue that a car is a more pressing need. In this essay, I will examine the arguments for both sides and provide a conclusion on which option is the better choice.

One argument in favour of buying a house first is that it is a more stable and long-term investment. Unlike cars, which depreciate in value over time, a house has the potential to increase in value over time. Additionally, owning a house can provide a sense of security and stability, as it can serve as a permanent residence and provide a space to call your own. This can be especially important for those looking to start a family or build roots in a community.

Another argument in favour of buying a house first is that it is more cost-effective in the long run. Renting a house can be a constant drain on finances, as rent often increases over time. In contrast, paying a mortgage on a house can provide a sense of ownership and can ultimately lead to a lower overall cost. Additionally, paying off a mortgage can also provide a source of equity that can be used for future investments or financial security.

On the other hand, there are arguments in favour of buying a car first. One of these arguments is that a car is a more pressing need, as it provides the necessary transportation to get to and from work or other daily activities. Without a car, it can be difficult to get around and maintain a stable job, which can negatively impact financial stability.

Additionally, owning a car can provide a sense of independence and freedom, as it eliminates the need for public transportation or ride-sharing services.

Another argument in favour of buying a car first is that it may be easier to obtain financing for a car than a house. This can be especially true for those with limited credit history or those who may not yet be in a position to take on a mortgage. In contrast, buying a house may require a larger down payment and a more significant financial commitment.

To wrap things up, whether to buy a house or a car first is a personal decision that depends on an individual's financial situation and priorities. While buying a house can provide long-term stability and cost-effectiveness, buying a car can provide necessary transportation and independence. Ultimately, it is important to consider one's financial goals and needs, as well as the current market conditions, when making the decision on which option to choose.

The Debate Over Teen Relationships: To Be or Not to Be in Love Before College

Teenage years are often associated with the discovery of love, self-identity and exploration of personal relationships. Some argue that teenagers should be encouraged to pursue romantic relationships and learn about love and relationships at a young age, while others believe that it is better for teenagers to wait until after college before entering into a relationship. In this essay, I will argue that the decision to be in a relationship as a teenager should be based on individual circumstances and not a universal rule.

On the one hand, being in a relationship as a teenager can be beneficial for personal growth and development. It can help teenagers learn about communication, commitment and the importance of compromise in a relationship. These skills and experiences can be valuable for their future relationships and personal lives. Additionally, being in a relationship can provide teenagers with a sense of emotional support and stability during a time when they are experiencing rapid changes and challenges.

However, some argue that being in a relationship during the teenage years can be a distraction from academic and personal goals. Teenagers are at a critical stage in their lives where they are forming their identities and making important decisions about their future. The demands of a relationship can take time away from academics and personal growth, potentially impacting their future success and happiness.

Furthermore, teenagers are still developing their emotional and psychological maturity, which can lead to impulsive and unhealthy relationships. The emotional intensity of teenage relationships can also lead to heartbreak and negative consequences, which can affect mental health and future relationships.

The bottom line is this. The decision to be in a relationship as a teenager should be based on individual circumstances and not a universal rule. While being in a relationship can provide benefits for personal growth and development, it can also be a distraction from academics and personal goals. Teenagers need to consider their priorities and assess whether a relationship aligns with their current goals and aspirations. Ultimately, the decision should be made based on the teenager's unique needs and circumstances, with the goal of promoting their overall happiness and success.

Saving for a House or for Adventure: Which is More Important?

In today's world, many young people face the dilemma of choosing between saving for their first home or setting aside money for travel. On one hand, owning a home is often seen as a symbol of stability and financial security. On the other hand, travel is a way to explore the world and experience new cultures, which can be an enriching and life-changing experience. In this essay, I will argue that while both options have their merits, saving for travel is more important in the long run.

One of the main arguments in favour of saving for travel is that it provides us with experiences that are not only enriching but also unique and unforgettable. When we travel, we get to see new places, meet new people, and try new things that we would never have the opportunity to do if we were simply focused on saving for a house. These experiences broaden our horizons and give us a new perspective on life, making us more confident, open-minded, and culturally aware.

Another argument in favour of travel is that it can be an opportunity for personal growth and development. When we step out of our comfort zones and experience new things, we challenge ourselves and learn more about who we are and what we want from life. This can be especially important for young people who are just starting out on their life journeys, as it can help them to establish a sense of purpose and direction.

In contrast, saving for a house is seen as more practical and secure. Owning a home is often seen as a long-term investment that can provide financial stability and a secure place to live. However, it is important to consider that a house is not just a financial investment but also a commitment to one specific location. If we focus solely on saving for a house, we may miss out on opportunities to explore other parts of the world and experience new cultures, which can limit our personal growth and broaden our perspectives.

Furthermore, while buying a house is a significant financial investment, it is not the only option for securing our financial futures. There are many other ways to invest our money, such as stocks, bonds, or mutual funds, which can provide similar financial benefits without tying us down to one specific location.

To summarize, while saving for a house can provide financial stability and a secure place to live, saving for travel is more important in the long run. Travel provides us with unique and unforgettable experiences, as well as opportunities for personal growth and development. While buying a house is a significant investment, there are other ways to invest our money, so it is important to strike a balance between practical considerations and the desire for adventure.

Staying Abroad vs. Staying Local: A Comparison of Life Choices

In today's interconnected world, more and more people have the opportunity to live and work abroad. This has led to a growing debate about the benefits and drawbacks of staying abroad versus staying local. On one hand, staying abroad offers the opportunity to experience new cultures, expand one's horizons, and meet new people. On the other hand, staying local provides a sense of stability, familiarity, and community. In this essay, I will compare the pros and cons of staying abroad versus staying local, and argue that the best choice depends on one's individual circumstances and priorities.

One of the main advantages of staying abroad is the opportunity to experience new cultures and ways of life. This can broaden one's perspectives and help to develop a more open-minded and tolerant outlook. In addition, staying abroad provides the chance to meet new people from diverse backgrounds, which can lead to new friendships and valuable connections. Furthermore, staying abroad can also offer new job opportunities and professional growth, as well as the chance to learn new languages and skills.

However, staying abroad also comes with its own set of challenges and drawbacks. For one, it can be difficult to adapt to a new culture, especially if the language and customs are significantly different from one's own. Additionally, staying abroad can be expensive, especially if one is not familiar with the local cost of living. Furthermore, staying abroad can also be lonely, as it can be hard to maintain relationships with friends and family who are far away.

In contrast, staying local offers the benefits of stability, familiarity, and community. For example, staying local allows one to be close to friends and family, which can provide a sense of security and support.

Additionally, staying local can also be less expensive, as one is familiar with the cost of living and local resources. Furthermore, staying local can provide opportunities for personal and professional growth, as one has access to a familiar network of resources and support.

At the end of the day, the choice between staying abroad and staying local depends on one's individual circumstances and priorities. Both options have their pros and cons, and what works best for one person may not work for another. Ultimately, it is up to each individual to weigh the benefits and drawbacks of each option and make the best decision for themselves.

Studying Locally or Studying Abroad

Studying locally or studying abroad is a common decision faced by many students as they begin to think about their future education and career prospects. Both options have their own advantages and disadvantages, and ultimately, the decision comes down to personal preferences and circumstances. In this essay, I will argue that while both options have their merits, studying abroad offers greater opportunities and benefits, and should be considered as a viable option for students.

One of the key benefits of studying abroad is the exposure to a new culture and way of life. Studying in a foreign country provides students with the opportunity to immerse themselves in a new environment and experience different customs, traditions, and ways of thinking. This exposure to diversity can help students to become more open-minded and culturally aware, which can be valuable in their personal and professional lives.

Another advantage of studying abroad is the opportunity to improve language skills. For students who want to study in a foreign language, studying abroad provides an immersive and intensive language learning experience that is not possible in a local setting. Furthermore, speaking and using a foreign language on a daily basis can significantly improve fluency and comprehension.

Moreover, studying abroad can also provide students with access to a wider range of educational resources and opportunities. Many universities abroad have cutting-edge facilities, world-class faculty, and research programs that are not available in the local setting. This can provide students with an advantage when it comes to pursuing advanced degrees or embarking on a research career.

However, it's important to consider that studying abroad can also be more challenging and expensive than studying locally. Living and studying in a foreign country can be difficult, as students may face cultural differences, language barriers, and homesickness. In addition, the cost of tuition, living expenses, and travel can be significantly higher when studying abroad.

In conclusion, while studying locally has its advantages, such as convenience and lower costs, studying abroad offers greater opportunities for personal and academic growth. By exposing students to a new culture, improving language skills, and providing access to world-class resources, studying abroad can provide a unique and valuable experience that is not possible in a local setting. Therefore, students should seriously consider studying abroad as a viable option for their future education and career prospects.

The Pros and Cons of Working a Day Shift vs a Night Shift

The debate about whether to work a day shift or a night shift is a common one, with each option having its own pros and cons. On one hand, day shifts offer the benefits of a more conventional schedule, which can be helpful for maintaining a healthy work-life balance. On the other hand, night shifts offer the potential for increased pay and a more flexible schedule, which can be ideal for those who prefer to sleep during the day.

One of the main advantages of working a day shift is that it aligns with the conventional schedule most people follow. This makes it easier to maintain a healthy work-life balance, as well as to engage in social and recreational activities outside of work. It also allows for a better sleep pattern, which is crucial for maintaining good health and overall well-being.

However, the biggest disadvantage of working a day shift is that it is typically less well-paying than a night shift. This is because day shift workers often compete with a larger pool of candidates, and there is often a greater demand for these positions. As a result, many people who prefer day shifts are forced to accept lower wages or work in lower-skilled positions.

On the other hand, working a night shift can offer several advantages, including higher pay, a more flexible schedule, and the potential for increased job security. Night shift workers are often able to command higher wages because there is a lower supply of workers willing to work these hours. Additionally, night shift work can be ideal for those who prefer to sleep during the day, as they can take advantage of the time to rest and recharge.

However, working a night shift can also have several negative impacts on a person's health and well-being. Night shift work is often associated with disrupted sleep patterns, which can lead to a range of health problems, including fatigue, insomnia, and depression. Additionally, night shift workers are often isolated from friends and family, which can be lonely and isolating.

To conclude, whether to work a day shift or a night shift is a personal decision that depends on a person's individual circumstances and priorities. Those who value a more conventional schedule and a better work-life balance may prefer working a day shift, while those who are looking for higher pay and a more flexible schedule may prefer working a night shift. Ultimately, the decision should be based on careful consideration of the pros and cons of each option, and what will work best for each individual.

The Debate Over Having Children: To Give Birth or Not to Give Birth

Having children is one of the most significant decisions that a person can make, and it is not surprising that there is a lot of debate about whether or not it is the right choice for everyone. On one hand, there are those who believe that having children is an essential part of life and that it brings joy and meaning to their lives. On the other hand, there are those who believe that choosing not to have children is the better option, as it allows them to focus on other aspects of their lives and pursue their own interests and goals.

One argument in favour of having children is that it provides a sense of purpose and fulfilment. For many people, having children is a natural and instinctual desire, and they feel that it is an essential part of their life journey. Raising a family can bring a sense of joy, fulfilment, and pride, and it is an opportunity to leave a lasting legacy and make a positive impact on the world.

Another argument in favour of having children is that it can provide a sense of community and belonging. Children bring families together and create a network of support and love that can last a lifetime. Having children can also bring a sense of responsibility and purpose, as parents work to provide for and protect their children.

On the other hand, some people argue that choosing not to have children is the better option. For these individuals, having children is not a priority, and they believe that it would interfere with other aspects of their life, such as their career, personal growth, and freedom. Additionally, not having children can provide a sense of financial stability and freedom, as it eliminates the costs and responsibilities of raising a family.

Another argument against having children is the potential impact on the environment. The global population is growing rapidly, and many experts believe that this growth is having a significant impact on the planet. By choosing not to have children, individuals can help reduce the strain on the planet's resources and reduce their own environmental footprint.

To wrap things up, the decision of whether or not to have children is a highly personal one, and there are compelling arguments on both sides. Whether a person chooses to have children or not, it is important that they make this decision based on their own values, goals, and priorities, and that they do so with a full understanding of the potential benefits and drawbacks of each option.

Controlling Population Size: Balancing the Interests of Society and Individual Freedoms

In today's world, overpopulation has become a pressing issue, with many countries struggling to provide adequate resources for their growing populations. In response, some argue that it is necessary to implement measures to control population size in order to ensure the sustainability of our planet and improve quality of life for future generations. However, others believe that this violates individual freedoms and could have unintended consequences.

On the one hand, proponents of population control argue that overpopulation puts a strain on natural resources and contributes to environmental degradation. By reducing population size, we can reduce the demand for these resources, conserve them for future generations, and mitigate the impacts of climate change. Additionally, by controlling population size, governments can ensure that the necessary resources are available to provide essential services, such as healthcare and education, to their citizens.

However, critics argue that measures to control population size are often intrusive and violate individual rights. For example, mandatory birth control or forced sterilization are unethical and could lead to a decrease in the quality of life for individuals. Additionally, some argue that population control measures often target marginalized communities, leading to further discrimination and inequality.

Another concern is that population control measures may have unintended consequences. For example, reducing population size may lead to an aging population and a shrinking workforce, which could have negative impacts on the economy. Additionally, population control measures may discourage immigration, leading to a decrease in cultural diversity and limiting the exchange of ideas and perspectives.

To summarize, the issue of overpopulation and population control is a complex and controversial one, with valid arguments on both sides. While reducing population size may provide benefits for the environment and ensure that resources are available for future generations, it also raises important ethical questions and has the potential for unintended consequences. Ultimately, the decision to control population size should be based on a careful consideration of both the benefits and the risks, and must strike a balance between the interests of society and the rights of individuals.

The Ethics of Cloning: To Clone or Not to Clone?

In recent years, the development of cloning technology has sparked a heated debate about the ethics of human and animal cloning. While some see it as a potential solution to infertility, disease, and even death, others believe that it is unethical and raises serious moral and scientific concerns.

On the one hand, proponents of cloning argue that it offers numerous benefits for society. For example, cloning could be used to cure genetic diseases by producing identical cells that could be used to replace diseased cells. Additionally, cloning could help to address infertility by allowing infertile couples to have children that are genetically related to them. Some also argue that cloning could help to extend human life by allowing us to produce replacement parts for our bodies when they start to wear out.

However, opponents of cloning argue that it is an unethical practice that poses a threat to the sanctity of human life. They argue that cloning is a form of manipulation that reduces human beings to mere commodities, and that it raises serious questions about the value and dignity of human life. Furthermore, there are concerns about the safety and welfare of cloned animals and humans, as well as the potential for abuse and exploitation.

Another concern is the impact that cloning could have on the diversity of life. If cloning becomes widespread, it could lead to a reduction in genetic diversity, which could have serious consequences for the health and survival of our species. Additionally, some argue that cloning represents a major step towards a Brave New World-style dystopia where people are manufactured to meet specific needs, rather than born with their own unique personalities and traits.

In conclusion, the ethics of cloning are complex and multi-faceted, and there are valid arguments on both sides. While it is clear that cloning offers numerous potential benefits, it is also important to consider the ethical and moral implications of this technology. Before we rush to embrace cloning, we must carefully consider the impact that it could have on society, the environment, and the very essence of what it means to be human.

The Benefits and Risks of Taking Supplements: A Case for Evidence-Based Decision Making

In today's society, supplements have become a popular and readily accessible option for individuals looking to improve their health and wellness. With a wide range of options available, from vitamins and minerals to herbal remedies and protein powders, it can be tempting to start taking supplements without fully understanding their effects and benefits. However, this raises important questions about the safety and efficacy of these products and whether they are truly necessary.

On one hand, proponents of supplements argue that they can provide numerous benefits, including improved overall health, enhanced athletic performance, and reduced risk of disease. For example, some studies have shown that taking vitamin and mineral supplements can help improve immune function, reduce oxidative stress, and lower the risk of chronic diseases like heart disease and cancer.

However, it is important to note that not all supplements are created equal and that some may have negative effects or interact with other medications. For example, taking high doses of certain vitamins, such as Vitamin A and Vitamin E, can have toxic effects, while herbal supplements may interact with prescription medications.

Furthermore, many of the benefits claimed by supplement manufacturers are not supported by scientific evidence. While some supplements may have some positive effects, it is important to consider the quality and reliability of the research behind these claims. In many cases, the studies used to support the benefits of supplements are poorly designed or have limited sample sizes, making it difficult to draw firm conclusions about their effectiveness.

In light of these concerns, it is important for individuals to make informed and evidence-based decisions about taking supplements. This means considering the risks and benefits, consulting with healthcare professionals, and carefully reviewing the scientific evidence behind each product.

In a nutshell, while supplements may have some benefits, it is important to consider the risks and make informed decisions based on evidence. By taking a holistic approach to health and wellness, individuals can ensure they are taking the best steps towards a healthier and happier life.

The Great Debate: To Watch in Cinema or At Home – Which Offers the Ultimate Movie Experience?

In today's world, technology has made it possible for us to watch movies in the comfort of our own homes. With the advent of streaming services like Netflix, Hulu, and Amazon Prime, we can now watch our favourite movies and TV shows from the comfort of our couch. On the other hand, watching movies in a cinema is still a popular activity and provides an entirely different experience. In this essay, we will explore the pros and cons of both options to determine which offers the ultimate movie experience.

One argument in favour of watching movies in a cinema is that it provides a communal experience. When we watch movies in a cinema, we are surrounded by other people, and this can be a very social and enjoyable experience. This sense of community can add to the overall enjoyment of the movie, making it a much more memorable experience.

Another argument in favour of watching movies in a cinema is the high-quality sound and visual effects. Cinemas are equipped with state-of-the-art sound systems and high-definition projectors, which provide an immersive experience that is difficult to replicate at home. The large screen and high-quality sound system can also make the movie feel more intense and impactful, allowing us to get fully absorbed in the story.

On the other hand, watching movies at home has its own set of advantages. One of the main advantages is the convenience and comfort that it provides. We can pause the movie whenever we want, and we can also watch it in our pyjamas or even in bed, making the experience much more relaxed and comfortable. In addition, home theatres are becoming increasingly popular, and with the right equipment, we can now get a movie experience that is almost as good as going to the cinema.

Another advantage of watching movies at home is the cost. The cost of watching movies in a cinema can quickly add up, especially if you are watching with friends or family. In contrast, watching movies at home is often much more affordable, as we only need to pay for the cost of the movie or the monthly subscription for a streaming service.

The bottom line is this. Whether it is watching in a cinema or at home, both options have their own advantages and disadvantages. While watching movies in a cinema provides a communal experience and high-quality sound and visual effects, watching movies at home offers the convenience and comfort of your own home, as well as cost savings. Ultimately, the choice between watching in a cinema or at home comes down to personal preference, and both options can provide a great movie experience.

The Illusion of a Better Life Abroad: Is the Grass Always Greener Overseas?

In today's globalized world, many people are tempted to look overseas for better opportunities and a higher standard of living. The idea of a better life abroad is often fuelled by media portrayals and personal anecdotes, leading many to believe that the grass truly is greener on the other side. However, this is not always the case. While there may be certain advantages to living abroad, there are also many downsides to consider.

One of the key reasons why people move overseas is for the promise of better job opportunities and higher salaries. However, while the initial financial benefits may be attractive, they often come at a cost. Moving to a foreign country can be expensive, and the cost of living can be much higher than what people are used to in their home country. This can lead to a lower standard of living, despite the higher salary.

Furthermore, moving to a foreign country can also result in social isolation and loneliness. Even in countries where the local population is welcoming, it can be difficult to establish meaningful relationships with new people. This can result in feelings of loneliness and homesickness, which can negatively impact one's well-being.

Another factor to consider is cultural differences. While living in a foreign country can be a unique and enriching experience, it can also be a source of stress and discomfort. Different cultural norms and customs can be challenging to adjust to, and language barriers can further exacerbate these difficulties.

In conclusion, while the idea of a better life abroad may seem tempting, it is important to consider the potential downsides. While there may be certain advantages to living abroad, such as better job opportunities and higher salaries, these benefits often come at a cost. Moving to a foreign country can result in financial strain, social isolation, cultural differences, and other challenges that can negatively impact one's well-being. Ultimately, the grass is not always greener overseas, and it is important to weigh the pros and cons before making a decision to move.

Agriculture vs. Manufacturing: Which Provides Greater Benefits to Our Country?

In today's fast-paced and ever-changing world, the question of which industry provides the greatest benefits to our country remains a topic of discussion and debate. On one hand, agriculture is seen as a vital sector that provides food, jobs, and economic stability to rural communities. On the other hand, manufacturing is seen as a key driver of technological advancement and economic growth, offering high-paying jobs and access to new products and services.

One argument in favour of agriculture is that it provides a sustainable source of food and raw materials. With the world's population growing at an unprecedented rate, the demand for food is increasing and agriculture has become an important means of meeting this demand. Agricultural products are also the basis for many other industries, such as the production of biofuels, textiles, and chemicals.

Another argument in favour of agriculture is that it provides a significant source of employment for rural communities. In many areas, agriculture is the primary employer and a major contributor to the local economy. It offers a range of job opportunities, from farming and production to marketing and distribution.

In contrast, the manufacturing industry is seen as a key driver of technological advancement and economic growth. It offers high-paying jobs in industries such as electronics, aerospace, and automotive, and provides access to new products and services that are critical to modern society. The manufacturing sector is also seen as a way of reducing dependence on imports and improving the balance of trade.

However, some argue that manufacturing also has negative impacts on the environment, including the release of pollutants and the consumption of finite resources. Additionally, manufacturing can lead to job losses in traditional industries as companies seek to reduce costs and improve efficiency.

At the end of the day, both agriculture and manufacturing have important roles to play in our country's economy. While agriculture provides a sustainable source of food and employment for rural communities, manufacturing drives technological advancement and economic growth. The most effective approach is to find a balance between the two, ensuring that each sector receives the support and investment it needs to succeed.

Selfish or Helpful: Debating the Nature of Humanity

In today's society, there is a growing perception that people are becoming increasingly selfish. From a lack of empathy in our politics and public discourse, to the seemingly endless pursuit of individual gain, it is easy to see why this perspective is becoming more widespread. On the other hand, there are those who argue that people are inherently helpful and that it is only our current environment and cultural norms that are driving us towards greater selfishness. In this essay, I will examine both sides of this debate and argue that while it is true that some people are more selfish than helpful, it is not accurate to make a blanket statement about all of humanity.

One of the arguments in favour of people being selfish is that our society rewards individualism and self-interest. The media glorifies wealth and success, and the focus on individual achievement has led many to prioritize their own interests over the needs of others. This can result in a lack of empathy and consideration for others, leading to a general sense that people are becoming more selfish.

On the other hand, there is evidence to suggest that people are naturally helpful and cooperative. For example, studies have shown that people are more likely to help others in emergency situations, and that people are generally more likely to be cooperative when they are in close relationships with others. Additionally, many people are involved in volunteer work or other forms of community service, which suggests that they have a strong desire to help others.

It is also important to consider the context in which people are acting. For example, in some cases, people may appear to be selfish when they are simply trying to protect their own interests. Similarly, in some cases, people may appear to be helpful when they are actually trying to advance their own goals. It is only by examining the specific context and motivations behind people's actions that we can truly determine whether they are selfish or helpful.

On the whole, the debate over whether people are becoming more selfish or helpful is a complex one. While it is true that some people are more selfish than helpful, it is not accurate to make a blanket statement about all of humanity. By examining the specific context and motivations behind people's actions, we can better understand the nature of humanity and the factors that contribute to selfish or helpful behaviour.

Weighing the Benefits and Burdens: The Conundrum of Helping Others

In today's society, there is a common belief that people are more selfish than helpful. However, the idea that helping others adds to one's own burden is a debatable topic. On one hand, some argue that helping others can be a burden as it takes time, effort, and resources that could be used for oneself. On the other hand, others believe that helping others can bring great joy and fulfilment and can have a positive impact on one's own life.

One argument in favour of helping others is that it can bring a sense of purpose and fulfilment. When we help others, we feel a sense of accomplishment and satisfaction knowing that we have made a difference in someone's life. This sense of purpose can lead to greater happiness and fulfilment and can improve one's own mental and emotional well-being.

Additionally, helping others can also bring a sense of community and connectedness. When we help others, we build relationships and connections with those around us. This sense of community and connectedness can lead to a greater sense of belonging and can help improve our own happiness and well-being.

Another argument in favour of helping others is that it can have a positive impact on our own lives. Research has shown that helping others can improve our own physical health, reduce stress and anxiety, and increase our own life satisfaction. When we help others, we engage in acts of kindness and generosity, which can improve our own mood and well-being.

However, it is also important to acknowledge that helping others can sometimes lead to feelings of burnout or overwhelm. When we take on too much, it can become overwhelming and lead to feelings of stress and exhaustion. In order to avoid this, it is important to find a balance between helping others and taking care of oneself.

When all things considered, while helping others can sometimes be seen as a burden, it is also important to acknowledge the many benefits that it can bring. Helping others can bring a sense of purpose and fulfilment, a sense of community and connectedness, and can have a positive impact on our own lives. It is important to find a balance between helping others and taking care of oneself to avoid feelings of burnout or overwhelm.

The Burden of Youth vs. Adulthood: Which Generation Faces More Challenges?

The question of whether young people or adults have more problems to deal with is a complex and subjective one. While young people often face challenges such as navigating their identities, building relationships, and preparing for the future, adults often confront difficulties like managing their finances, balancing work and family life, and coping with the physical and mental health issues that come with aging.

On the one hand, young people are often grappling with a multitude of emotional and psychological challenges as they make the transition from childhood to adulthood. They may struggle with anxiety and depression, peer pressure and bullying, and a lack of direction or purpose. In addition, young people are often expected to make decisions about their careers, education, and relationships at a time when they are still trying to figure out who they are. This can create a sense of overwhelm and uncertainty that can be challenging to manage.

On the other hand, adults are faced with a different set of problems, many of which are rooted in the challenges of balancing the demands of work and family. They may struggle to make ends meet financially, or find it difficult to manage the demands of a high-pressure job while maintaining meaningful relationships with their partners, children, and friends. Furthermore, as they age, they may be more likely to experience health problems, such as chronic illnesses and disabilities, that can impact their quality of life and ability to function.

It is worth noting, however, that the challenges faced by young people and adults are not mutually exclusive. Many adults struggle with the emotional and psychological issues that are common among young people, while many young people are already grappling with the financial, work-related, and health problems that are often associated with adulthood.

To wrap things up, both young people and adults face significant challenges in their lives, and it is difficult to say definitively which group has more problems to deal with. Ultimately, what matters most is that each individual is able to find support, guidance, and resources to help them overcome their difficulties and live a fulfilling life.

The Profit Motive in Professional Sports: Balancing Passion and Profit

The world of professional sports is a multi-billion-dollar industry, with top athletes earning millions of dollars in salaries and endorsement deals. However, as the stakes continue to rise, many argue that the focus of professional athletes has shifted away from the love of the game to the pursuit of financial gain. Critics argue that this emphasis on making money has led to a decrease in the quality of play, as well as a tarnished reputation for the sports industry as a whole.

On the one hand, it is understandable that professional athletes would want to maximize their earnings. They only have a limited time to make a career in sports and secure their financial future. Moreover, the high-pressure environment of professional sports often requires significant investments in training, equipment, and travel, which can place a strain on athletes' finances. By earning high salaries, athletes can offset these costs and provide for their families.

However, opponents argue that this focus on making money has come at the expense of the integrity of the game. Many argue that the emphasis on winning at all costs, rather than playing for the love of the sport, has led to unethical behaviour such as cheating and performance-enhancing drug use. This can result in a negative image for the sport, causing fans to lose faith in the athletes and the sport itself.

Additionally, some argue that the profit motive in professional sports is a prime example of the negative effects of capitalism on society. They believe that the focus on making money has created an imbalance in the distribution of wealth, as the top athletes earn astronomical salaries while many fans struggle to make ends meet.

In conclusion, the debate over the profit motive in professional sports is a complex one, with valid arguments on both sides. While it is important for professional athletes to earn a living and provide for themselves and their families, it is equally crucial to maintain the integrity and passion for the sport. The key to finding a balance is to ensure that the focus remains on playing the game to the best of one's ability, rather than solely on financial gain.

The Duality of Computers: Blessing or Burden?

Computers have become an integral part of our daily lives, and it's difficult to imagine a world without them. On one hand, computers have revolutionized the way we work, communicate, and access information. On the other hand, there is growing concern about the negative impacts of computers, such as addiction, social isolation, and job loss. In this essay, I will examine both the benefits and drawbacks of computers, and explore whether they are ultimately a blessing or a burden to society.

The first and most obvious benefit of computers is their ability to automate repetitive tasks and increase efficiency. For example, computers have made it easier for businesses to manage financial transactions, keep track of inventory, and analyse data. In addition, computers have revolutionized the way we communicate, allowing us to stay connected with friends and family across the world, and to access vast amounts of information at the click of a button.

However, the over-reliance on computers has led to a number of negative consequences. One of the most concerning is the loss of jobs as more and more tasks are automated. While computers may increase efficiency, they also displace workers, creating a new set of problems for individuals and communities. In addition, computers have been linked to a number of health problems, such as eye strain, back pain, and carpal tunnel syndrome, as well as psychological issues like addiction, anxiety, and depression.

Furthermore, computers have changed the way we interact with each other, leading to increased social isolation and decreased face-to-face communication. Many argue that computers are creating a more superficial, less meaningful form of interaction, where people are more likely to communicate through a screen than in person.

To summarize, it is clear that computers have both blessings and burdens. While they have revolutionized the way we work and communicate, they have also created new problems, such as job loss and social isolation. Ultimately, it is up to us as individuals and society to manage the impact of computers and ensure that they serve us, rather than the other way around.

The Significance of Elders in Society: Agree or Disagree?

The role of elders in society has been a topic of debate for many years. On one hand, some people believe that elders play a crucial role in society and hold valuable knowledge, experience, and wisdom that should be honoured and respected. On the other hand, others argue that the younger generation has surpassed the elders in many aspects and that it is time for the elder population to step aside and make way for the new generation.

The proponents of the first viewpoint argue that elders have a wealth of experience and knowledge that they can pass on to the younger generation. They have lived through significant historical events, and have seen the world change over time. This gives them a unique perspective and allows them to provide valuable insights into societal issues. Furthermore, elders are often seen as respected leaders and mentors in their communities, providing guidance and support to those around them.

On the other hand, those who disagree with the significance of elders in society argue that the younger generation is more technologically advanced and better equipped to deal with the challenges of the modern world. They believe that the younger generation is more capable of adapting to changing circumstances, and that their innovations and advancements will bring about a brighter future. They argue that the elder population is simply not able to keep up with the fast pace of modern society, and that it is time for them to step aside.

However, it is important to note that both the young and the old have unique strengths and weaknesses, and both play important roles in society. The young bring energy, creativity, and innovation, while the elders bring stability, wisdom, and a wealth of knowledge. Both generations can learn from each other and work together to create a better future.

The bottom line is this. Whether or not elders play an important role in society is subjective and open to interpretation. However, it is clear that both the young and the old have valuable contributions to make, and it is important to recognize and respect the contributions of both generations.

Should Entertainers Be Paid More Than Doctors?

The debate over which profession deserves more pay has been ongoing for years. On one hand, doctors save lives and provide critical medical services, while on the other hand, entertainers bring joy and excitement to people's lives. In this essay, we will examine both sides of this argument and determine if entertainers should be paid more than doctors.

One of the main arguments for why doctors should be paid more is that they provide critical medical services to the community. Doctors are trained professionals who are responsible for diagnosing and treating a wide range of illnesses and injuries. They are also responsible for performing life-saving procedures and surgeries that can literally mean the difference between life and death. In light of this, it is only right that doctors are paid a high salary, as they play a vital role in society and are essential for the wellbeing of individuals.

On the other hand, entertainers also play a significant role in society. They bring joy, excitement, and laughter to people's lives through their performances, be it in music, film, theatre, or any other form of entertainment. They help people escape from the stress and hardships of everyday life and provide a source of entertainment that is much needed in today's fast-paced world. In addition, entertainers have to work hard to perfect their craft and hone their skills, which is why they deserve to be paid a decent salary.

At the end of the day, both doctors and entertainers play important roles in society and both deserve to be paid fairly for their services. While doctors provide critical medical services, entertainers bring joy and excitement to people's lives. Ultimately, the amount of pay that someone should receive should be based on the value they bring to society and the level of expertise they possess. Therefore, it is not appropriate to say that one profession deserves more pay than the other, as both are equally important in their own way.

97

Working Mother or Stay-at-Home Mom: What's the Best Choice for New Mothers?

The debate over whether mothers should work or stay at home to take care of their new-borns has been ongoing for years. On one hand, working mothers argue that they need to provide financial support for their family, and that working gives them a sense of independence and fulfilment. On the other hand, stay-at-home mothers argue that they are the best caretakers for their children, and that they want to be there for every step of their development.

The truth is, there is no right or wrong answer. Both options have their advantages and disadvantages, and the choice ultimately comes down to the individual needs and circumstances of each family.

For working mothers, one of the biggest advantages is the financial support they are able to provide. With the cost of living constantly on the rise, it is often necessary for both parents to work in order to make ends meet. In addition, working can also provide a sense of purpose and identity for mothers, allowing them to pursue their passions and interests outside of the home.

However, working mothers also face many challenges, such as balancing their job responsibilities with the needs of their children. They may also experience guilt for not being there for their children as much as they would like, or feel the pressure to perform both at work and at home. Furthermore, relying on others for childcare can also be a source of worry, as mothers want to ensure that their children are receiving the best care possible.

For stay-at-home mothers, one of the biggest advantages is the opportunity to be there for every step of their children's development.

They are able to provide consistent, loving care, and can also be more involved in their children's education and activities. In addition, stay-at-home mothers often have more flexibility in their schedule, allowing them to be there for their children when they need them the most.

However, stay-at-home mothers may also face financial difficulties, as they are relying solely on their partner's income. They may also experience feelings of isolation, as they are not able to interact with other adults on a daily basis. Furthermore, stay-at-home mothers may also feel pressure to be perfect, as they are solely responsible for their children's well-being.

In conclusion, both working mothers and stay-at-home mothers face their own unique challenges. The choice between the two ultimately comes down to the individual needs and circumstances of each family. Whether it's financial stability, the opportunity to be there for every step of their children's development, or a sense of purpose and identity, each mother must weigh the pros and cons and make the best decision for herself and her family.

Freedom or Confinement: The Fate of Animals

The question of whether animals are meant to be free or confined to a space has been a topic of debate for many years. On one hand, proponents of animal rights argue that all creatures should have the right to live in their natural habitats, unencumbered by human intervention. On the other hand, proponents of animal confinement argue that certain species, especially domesticated animals, require care and protection that can only be provided in controlled environments.

The issue of animal confinement is a complex one, as it encompasses a wide range of species and living conditions. Some proponents argue that confining animals in zoos, for example, allows for the preservation of endangered species and provides educational opportunities for the public. Zoos also claim to provide animals with veterinary care and adequate living conditions that may be unavailable in their natural habitats. However, opponents argue that zoos do not provide a suitable habitat for animals and often result in poor health and behavioural issues.

Domesticated animals, such as livestock and pets, also face a unique set of challenges. On the one hand, they are often confined in pens, cages, or kennels in order to protect them from predators and provide them with food and water. On the other hand, opponents argue that confining these animals can result in poor health and behavioural issues and that they should be allowed to roam freely.

To conclude, the answer to whether animals are meant to be free or confined is not a simple one. It depends on the specific species and their individual needs. In some cases, confinement may be necessary for the preservation of endangered species or for the protection of domesticated animals. However, it is important to ensure that any form of confinement provides animals with adequate living conditions and protection from harm.

Tradition vs Modernity: A Debate on Dress

In today's society, there is a constant debate between tradition and modernity, especially when it comes to the way we dress. On one hand, traditional dress is seen as a symbol of cultural heritage and a connection to our roots. It reflects the values and beliefs of a community and can bring a sense of pride and unity. On the other hand, modern dress is seen as a symbol of progress and freedom. It represents the breaking of traditional norms and the embracing of new, more progressive ways of thinking.

Those who advocate for traditional dress argue that it is important to preserve cultural identity and tradition, and that wearing traditional attire can help keep cultural heritage alive. They believe that traditional dress should be worn not only on special occasions, but also in everyday life. By doing so, younger generations can learn about their cultural heritage and pass it down to future generations.

On the other hand, proponents of modern dress argue that it represents freedom and the ability to express one's individuality. They believe that people should be able to wear what they want and not be limited by traditional norms. In addition, modern dress is often seen as more practical and comfortable, especially in a fast-paced, modern society where comfort is key.

Another point of view is that both traditional and modern dress have their place in society. Traditional dress can be worn for special events and celebrations, while modern dress can be worn in everyday life. This way, people can have the best of both worlds - they can preserve their cultural heritage and values through traditional dress, while also expressing their individuality and embracing progress through modern dress.

Ultimately, whether one should choose traditional or modern dress is a personal decision that depends on an individual's beliefs, values, and cultural background. Both have their benefits and drawbacks, and it is up to each person to decide what is best for them. However, it is important to recognize and respect the role that both traditional and modern dress play in society, and to see the value in preserving cultural heritage and traditions, while also embracing progress and change.

Enjoying Your Job vs. Earning Money: Which is More Important?

In today's society, people face many different choices and decisions that can impact their lives. One of the most common debates is whether enjoying one's job is more important than earning money, or vice versa. In this essay, we will explore both sides of this argument, in order to come to a conclusion about which is truly more important.

On one hand, there are many people who believe that earning money is the most important factor in a job. They argue that money provides stability and security, and allows individuals to live a comfortable lifestyle, take care of their families, and save for the future. For these people, a job is simply a means to an end, and the focus is on financial security, rather than personal satisfaction.

On the other hand, there are those who believe that enjoying one's job is the most important factor in a career. They argue that a job that is enjoyable provides individuals with a sense of purpose and fulfilment, and that this can contribute to a better overall quality of life. These people believe that happiness at work leads to better job performance, stronger relationships with colleagues, and a more positive outlook on life in general.

In short, whether earning money or enjoying one's job is more important depends on the individual, and there is no right or wrong answer to this question. When all things considered, the most important thing is to find a balance that works for you, and to make sure that your job is something that you are passionate about, and that provides you with a sense of satisfaction and purpose.

Education or Military: Where Should the Government Allocate Its Resources?

In today's world, both education and military hold significant importance in shaping the future of a country. The government must make crucial decisions on where to allocate its resources, and this has sparked a long-standing debate on whether education or military should receive more funding. In this essay, I will present arguments from both sides of the debate and state my position on the matter.

On the one hand, supporters of increasing the military budget argue that national security is a top priority and a strong military is crucial in protecting the country's interests. A well-equipped military force is essential in deterring threats and maintaining peace, and in times of conflict, a strong military can help bring stability and peace. The military also plays a significant role in safeguarding the country's borders and ensuring the safety of its citizens.

However, opponents of this argument believe that investing in education is just as important, if not more, as investing in the military. Education is essential in providing citizens with the skills and knowledge they need to succeed in life. It helps create a well-educated workforce that can drive innovation and economic growth. Additionally, investing in education has been proven to reduce poverty and increase economic equality, which ultimately benefits the entire society.

Furthermore, education has a more long-term impact on a country compared to the military. While the military can protect the country in the short term, it is education that has the potential to shape the future of a country by providing its citizens with the necessary tools to succeed. A well-educated population can drive progress and lead to a better future for all.

When all things considered, I believe that both education and military are crucial in shaping the future of a country and both should receive adequate funding. However, the government should focus on creating a balanced budget that prioritizes education over military spending. A strong education system will not only produce a well-informed and well-equipped population, but it will also create a sustainable future for the country.

Active Population Control: Necessity or Infringement?

The issue of population control has been a topic of debate for many years. While some believe that a country's population should be actively controlled in order to maintain economic stability and preserve resources, others argue that this approach infringes on individual freedoms and basic human rights.

On one hand, proponents of active population control argue that a growing population can lead to a strain on resources, including food, water, and housing. This can result in increased poverty and environmental degradation, leading to a decline in overall quality of life. Moreover, with a growing population, the government must allocate more resources towards healthcare, education, and social services, which can put a strain on the economy.

On the other hand, opponents of active population control argue that it is a violation of individual freedoms and basic human rights. Decisions about family planning should be left up to the individual, not the government. Additionally, population control policies have been criticized for their unequal and discriminatory application, with low-income and minority populations often bearing the brunt of these measures.

Furthermore, some argue that population control policies are not a sustainable solution to the problem of overpopulation. Instead, it is more important to focus on improving living conditions and increasing access to education and healthcare, which can help reduce the birth rate naturally over time.

On the whole, the issue of active population control is a complex and controversial one. While there may be benefits to controlling population growth, it must be done in a way that respects individual freedoms and basic human rights. Rather than implementing population control policies, a more sustainable solution may be to focus on improving living conditions and increasing access to education and healthcare.

The Pros and Cons of Being an Only Child or Having Siblings: Which is Better?

The age-old question of whether it is better to be an only child or have siblings has been a topic of debate for many years. While some argue that being an only child has its advantages, others believe that having siblings provides a more well-rounded upbringing. Both sides have valid arguments, and it ultimately depends on the individual and their unique circumstances.

One argument in favour of being an only child is that they receive more attention and resources from their parents. This can result in a more stable and secure childhood, with their parents' undivided love and attention. Additionally, only children often have more opportunities for individual activities, such as music lessons or sports teams, allowing them to develop their skills and interests to a greater extent.

On the other hand, having siblings can provide a wealth of benefits for children. Siblings provide a sense of companionship and camaraderie, helping to create a close-knit bond that can last a lifetime. Furthermore, growing up with siblings can help children develop social skills, empathy, and conflict resolution skills, which can be beneficial throughout their lives.

In terms of academic and personal growth, studies have shown that children who grow up with siblings tend to perform better academically and have better mental health outcomes compared to only children. Additionally, siblings can also provide support and guidance as children grow into adulthood.

To conclude, whether it is better to be an only child or have siblings is a subjective matter that depends on the individual's circumstances and experiences. However, both options have their pros and cons, and it is important to consider the potential impact on a child's upbringing when making this decision. Ultimately, it is the love and support of family that is most important, regardless of family size.

The Pros and Cons of Traditional Schools vs Home-School Education: A Personal Decision

The debate over whether students should attend traditional schools or receive a home-school education is a long-standing one that has been the subject of much discussion. Both options have their pros and cons, and the decision of which one to choose ultimately comes down to individual preference and circumstances.

On one hand, attending traditional schools provides students with the opportunity to socialize with their peers and develop a strong support network. This can be especially beneficial for introverted or shy children, as it can help them to break out of their shell and develop important social skills. Traditional schools also offer a wider range of subjects and activities, as well as access to professional teachers and facilities, which can help to broaden a student's knowledge and skills.

On the other hand, home-schooling offers several benefits that traditional schools do not. For example, it allows for a much more individualized and personalized education, as students can work at their own pace and focus on the subjects that interest them the most. Additionally, it allows parents to have a greater say in the type of education their children receive, and can help to create a closer bond between parent and child.

At the end of the day, the choice between attending traditional schools and receiving a home-school education is a personal one that depends on a variety of factors. Both options have their advantages and disadvantages, and it is up to each individual to weigh the pros and cons and choose the one that is best suited to their needs and circumstances.

The Ethics of Lying: Is Deception Ever Justified?

The question of whether lies can be acceptable is a complex one, as it touches upon several ethical, moral, and philosophical issues. On one hand, lying can often result in negative consequences, such as damaging relationships, loss of trust, and the perpetuation of falsehoods. On the other hand, there are situations in which lying may be seen as necessary or even desirable, such as in cases of self-defence or when protecting someone else's feelings.

One of the key arguments against lying is that it goes against the principles of honesty and truthfulness, which are considered fundamental values in many societies. When people lie, they deceive others and violate the trust that is placed in them, which can have lasting consequences for their relationships and reputation. In addition, lies can lead to the spread of false information and misinformation, which can have serious consequences for individuals and society as a whole.

However, there are also arguments in favour of lying-in certain situations. For example, some might argue that lying can be acceptable in cases where it serves a greater good, such as protecting someone from harm or preserving national security. In such cases, the ends may be seen as justifying the means, and lying may be seen as a necessary evil.

Ultimately, the acceptability of lies is a complex and multifaceted issue that depends on many factors, including the context, the motives behind the lie, and the impact it has on others. While lying is generally considered unacceptable, there are situations in which it may be seen as necessary or desirable, and the decision of whether to lie in any given situation is definitely up to the individual.

Freedom of the Press: The Debate over Media Control

The topic of press freedom and the role of the media in society has been a hotly debated one for many years. On one hand, the press is seen as an essential component of a democratic society, as it provides citizens with access to important information and holds those in power accountable. On the other hand, some argue that the press should be subject to control in order to protect the public from the spread of misinformation or malicious reporting.

Those who argue in favour of press freedom argue that without it, citizens would be left in the dark about important events and issues, and would be unable to make informed decisions. They argue that the press must be free to investigate, report, and publish information without fear of censorship or retaliation, and that this is a key component of a free and democratic society.

On the other hand, those who argue for control over the press argue that it is important to ensure that the information that is disseminated to the public is accurate and free from malicious intent. They argue that certain types of reporting, such as the spread of false information or hate speech, can be harmful to society and must be subject to control.

In conclusion, the issue of press freedom and control is a complex one, and there are compelling arguments on both sides. Ultimately, it is up to society as a whole to weigh the benefits and drawbacks of press freedom and to decide on a balance that protects both the right of citizens to access information and the right of the public to be protected from harmful or malicious reporting.

The Importance of Wildlife Conservation: Protecting Our Natural Heritage

Wildlife is a vital component of the natural world, providing balance and diversity to ecosystems and supporting the survival of countless species, including our own. Despite its importance, wildlife is under threat from human activities, including habitat destruction, pollution, and overexploitation. In this essay, I will argue that preserving wildlife is not only crucial for maintaining biodiversity, but also essential for our own well-being and future survival.

On the one hand, preserving wildlife is important for maintaining biodiversity, which is the variety of life on earth. Biodiversity is crucial for the survival of ecosystems and the species that depend on them. Without it, ecosystems can become unstable and suffer from a loss of resilience, which can have serious consequences for the survival of both wildlife and humans. In addition, preserving wildlife is important for ensuring that future generations have the opportunity to experience and appreciate the beauty and wonder of the natural world.

However, there are those who argue that wildlife preservation is not a priority, and that economic development and human needs should take precedence. They argue that preserving wildlife is too costly and that resources could be better used elsewhere. Furthermore, some believe that wildlife conservation is unnecessary, as many species will inevitably become extinct as the result of natural processes.

In response, it can be argued that preserving wildlife is not just a matter of protecting biodiversity, but also a matter of ensuring our own well-being and survival. Wildlife provides numerous benefits to human society, including food, medicines, and other resources. Additionally, many species play important roles in regulating ecosystems, including pollination, pest control, and carbon sequestration. Without these services, human society would suffer significant harm.

Moreover, the costs of not preserving wildlife are much higher than the costs of conservation. The loss of biodiversity can lead to the loss of critical ecosystem services, which can have far-reaching and long-lasting impacts on human well-being. In addition, the extinction of species is a loss to human knowledge and culture, and cannot be undone.

To conclude, preserving wildlife is not only crucial for maintaining biodiversity, but also essential for our own well-being and future survival. While it may require significant investment and effort, the long-term benefits of conservation far outweigh the costs. By taking action to protect and preserve wildlife, we can ensure that our natural heritage is protected for future generations and that the benefits it provides are available for generations to come.

The Role of Political Parties in a Democracy

In a democratic society, political parties are often seen as the cornerstone of the political system. They provide a platform for citizens to voice their opinions, influence policy decisions, and hold elected officials accountable. However, on the contrary, some argue that political parties are a hindrance to the functioning of a true democracy.

On the one hand, political parties serve as a means for citizens to organize and advocate for their beliefs and interests. By aligning with a particular political party, individuals are able to pool their resources and exert more influence on the political process. This can result in a more representative government, as parties work to ensure that the policies they support are reflected in the actions of elected officials.

On the other hand, opponents of political parties argue that they are a barrier to genuine democratic representation. They claim that parties are more concerned with winning elections and maintaining power than with serving the best interests of the people. As a result, political parties are often accused of engaging in corrupt practices and engaging in political polarization, which can result in gridlock and inaction.

In addition, political parties are often criticized for being too beholden to wealthy donors and special interests. This can result in policies that prioritize the interests of the wealthy and powerful over the needs of ordinary citizens. Furthermore, the influence of money in politics can result in the erosion of democratic accountability, as elected officials become more concerned with pleasing their donors than representing the will of the people.

Despite these criticisms, it is important to remember that political parties play a critical role in shaping the direction of a democratic society. They provide a means for citizens to influence government policies and hold elected officials accountable. While it is true that political parties can sometimes be a hindrance to true democracy, it is on the contrary equally true that they are essential to the functioning of a representative and responsive political system.

As a conclusion, the role of political parties in a democracy is a complex and controversial issue. On the one hand, political parties serve as a means for citizens to organize and advocate for their beliefs and interests. On the other hand, they are often criticized for being a barrier to genuine democratic representation, engaging in corrupt practices, and being too beholden to wealthy donors and special interests. Ultimately, it is up to each individual to weigh the pros and cons and decide for themselves the role they believe political parties should play in a democratic society.

The Debate on Gun Control: Pro vs. Anti-Gun Advocates

The issue of gun control has been a contentious topic in the United States for decades, with advocates on both sides presenting compelling arguments. On one hand, supporters of gun control argue that stricter regulations and laws can help reduce the number of gun-related deaths and injuries. On the other hand, those who oppose gun control argue that the right to bear arms is enshrined in the Second Amendment of the U.S. Constitution and is an essential component of personal freedom.

On the side of gun control, proponents argue that the proliferation of firearms in society is a major contributor to the high rate of gun-related deaths and injuries. They point to countries with stricter gun laws, such as Japan and Australia, which have significantly lower rates of gun violence compared to the United States. Additionally, gun control supporters argue that it is simply too easy for dangerous individuals, such as convicted felons and individuals with mental illnesses, to obtain firearms. Stricter background checks and licensing requirements, they argue, can help prevent these individuals from accessing firearms and reduce the risk of gun violence.

However, those who oppose gun control argue that the right to bear arms is a fundamental right and a crucial component of personal freedom. They argue that the government has no right to restrict the ownership of firearms and that doing so would only leave law-abiding citizens vulnerable to attacks by criminals who will still have access to firearms. Furthermore, they argue that the presence of firearms in society can actually help reduce crime, as criminals will be deterred by the possibility of encountering armed citizens.

In conclusion, the debate on gun control is a complex and highly charged issue that elicits strong opinions from both sides. While supporters of gun control argue that stricter regulations and laws can help reduce gun violence, those who oppose gun control argue that the right to bear arms is an essential component of personal freedom. The reality, however, is likely to lie somewhere in between, with a need for a balanced approach that takes into account the rights of gun owners as well as the safety of society as a whole.

The Debate on Gun Control: Protecting the People or Infringing on Rights?

The issue of gun control has been a highly debated topic in the United States for decades. Proponents of gun control argue that it is necessary to regulate the sale and ownership of firearms in order to reduce gun violence and protect citizens from harm. On the other hand, opponents of gun control believe that it is an infringement on their constitutional right to bear arms, and that more restrictive laws will not necessarily lead to a decrease in violence.

Advocates for gun control point to the high rates of gun-related deaths and mass shootings in the United States as evidence for the need for stricter regulation. They argue that by implementing background checks, waiting periods, and other restrictions on the sale and ownership of firearms, the number of gun-related deaths and crimes can be reduced. In addition, they argue that the Second Amendment was written in a time when the most advanced weapons were muskets, and that it is not relevant in today's world where high-powered semi-automatic weapons are easily accessible.

However, opponents of gun control argue that the right to bear arms is a fundamental right guaranteed by the Second Amendment, and that any attempt to regulate or restrict it is a violation of the Constitution. They argue that the vast majority of gun owners are responsible and law-abiding citizens, and that restrictions on firearms will only impact the ability of law-abiding citizens to protect themselves, their families, and their property. Furthermore, they believe that the real issue is not the availability of firearms, but rather the social and cultural factors that lead to violence and crime.

In conclusion, the debate on gun control is a complex and contentious issue with valid arguments on both sides. While some argue that stricter regulation is necessary to reduce gun violence, others argue that it is a violation of their constitutional rights. It is important for the government and citizens to engage in an open and honest dialogue about this issue in order to find a solution that balances the need for public safety with the protection of individual rights.

Universal Healthcare: A Right or a Privilege?

The debate over whether or not universal healthcare should be a right or a privilege has been a hot topic for many years. Those in favour of universal healthcare argue that access to healthcare should be a basic human right, while those against it believe it should only be available to those who can afford it. In this essay, I will examine both sides of the argument and come to a conclusion about the future of healthcare in our society.

On one hand, supporters of universal healthcare argue that access to healthcare is a basic human right, just like access to food, shelter, and education. They argue that no one should have to go without medical treatment because they cannot afford it. They believe that the government has a responsibility to provide its citizens with access to quality healthcare, regardless of their income. This, they argue, will lead to a healthier society and a stronger economy in the long run.

On the contrary, opponents of universal healthcare believe that it should be a privilege, not a right. They argue that the government has no business being involved in healthcare, and that individuals should be responsible for their own healthcare. They believe that the cost of universal healthcare would be too high, and that it would lead to decreased quality of care. Furthermore, they argue that the government would have too much control over individuals' medical decisions, leading to a loss of personal freedom.

So, what is the answer? Should universal healthcare be a right or a privilege? In my opinion, the answer is clear: access to healthcare should be a basic human right. The benefits of universal healthcare far outweigh the potential costs and drawbacks. A healthy society is a productive society, and ensuring that all citizens have access to quality healthcare will lead to a stronger, more resilient society in the long run.

In conclusion, while there are certainly valid arguments on both sides of the debate over universal healthcare, it is my belief that access to healthcare should be considered a basic human right. Providing all citizens with access to quality healthcare will lead to a healthier, stronger society in the long run. To achieve this goal, we must work together to find ways to make universal healthcare a reality for all.

The Impact of Technology on Society: Blessing or Curse?

In recent years, technology has rapidly advanced and become an integral part of our daily lives. From smartphones and laptops to smart homes and self-driving cars, it is clear that technology has had a profound impact on our society. However, the question remains: is this impact a blessing or a curse?

On one hand, technology has brought about numerous benefits to our lives. For example, it has made communication faster and easier, providing instant access to information and connecting people from all over the world. In addition, technology has revolutionized industries such as medicine and education, making treatments and learning more efficient and accessible. Moreover, technological advancements have helped create new jobs and opportunities, boosting economic growth and reducing poverty.

However, there are also some negative consequences that cannot be ignored. For example, technology has led to increased social isolation and loneliness, as people spend more time staring at screens and less time interacting with each other. Additionally, technology has contributed to the loss of privacy and security, as sensitive personal information is collected and stored by corporations and governments. Furthermore, the dependence on technology has raised concerns about job security, as machines and algorithms replace human labour.

To summarize, the impact of technology on society is complex and multifaceted. While it has certainly brought about many benefits, it has also created new challenges and problems. In the end, it is up to us to ensure that technology is used for the betterment of society, rather than to its detriment. By being mindful of the impact of technology and making informed decisions, we can create a future that is both technologically advanced and socially responsible.

The Importance of Public Funding for the Arts

Art has always been an essential part of human culture, reflecting our beliefs, values, and experiences. From paintings to sculptures, from music to theatre, art has the power to inspire, challenge, and entertain us. Despite its importance, however, public funding for the arts is often seen as a luxury that can be easily cut during times of economic hardship.

On the one hand, some argue that the arts should be funded privately, through individual donations and corporate sponsorships. They argue that the government should not be responsible for funding the arts and that private funding would provide more accountability and flexibility for the arts community. They claim that private funding would allow artists and arts organizations to pursue their creative visions without interference from government bureaucracies.

On the contrary, however, it is clear that private funding alone cannot support the arts on a large scale. While individual donations and corporate sponsorships are important, they are often limited in their scope and cannot provide the consistent and reliable funding that the arts need to thrive. Furthermore, the arts have an important role to play in our society and should be accessible to everyone, not just those who can afford to pay for it.

Public funding for the arts provides a more equitable and sustainable solution. By providing stable and consistent funding, the government can ensure that the arts are available to everyone, regardless of their economic status. This can help to promote cultural diversity and support the arts in communities that may not otherwise have access to it. Furthermore, public funding can help to support the development of new and innovative art forms, promoting cultural and creative growth.

In short, while some may argue that the arts should be funded privately, the reality is that public funding is essential to ensuring that the arts continue to play a vital role in our society. From promoting cultural diversity to supporting creative growth, public funding for the arts is an investment in our future and in the cultural heritage of our nation.

The Case for Raising the Minimum Wage

The debate over minimum wage has been a controversial issue for decades, with arguments for and against a raise in the minimum wage being passionately debated. On one hand, supporters of increasing the minimum wage argue that it is necessary to help low-wage workers make ends meet and reduce poverty. On the contrary, opponents argue that increasing the minimum wage will lead to job losses and higher prices for consumers.

The current minimum wage in the United States is $7.25 per hour, which has remained unchanged since 2009. This means that millions of workers are earning wages that are far below what is needed to support themselves and their families. The cost of living has increased significantly over the years, and many minimum-wage workers are struggling to make ends meet. They are forced to rely on government assistance programs and other forms of support, which is not sustainable in the long term.

Raising the minimum wage would provide a much-needed boost to these workers and help them to become more self-sufficient. This would lead to reduced poverty, improved health outcomes, and increased economic growth. Additionally, raising the minimum wage would provide a boost to local economies as low-wage workers would have more disposable income to spend on goods and services. This would lead to increased demand for goods and services, which would, in turn, create jobs and stimulate economic growth.

On the contrary, opponents argue that increasing the minimum wage will lead to job losses and higher prices for consumers. They argue that businesses will have to reduce the number of employees they hire or reduce the hours that their employees work in order to absorb the increased labour costs. Additionally, businesses may also increase prices for goods and services, which will result in inflation and higher costs for consumers.

However, these arguments are based on outdated economic models and have been debunked by numerous studies. In fact, many studies have shown that raising the minimum wage has little to no impact on job losses and does not result in higher prices for consumers. Furthermore, many businesses have found that paying their employees a fair wage actually results in increased productivity, lower turnover, and reduced absenteeism.

In short, raising the minimum wage is not only necessary to help low-wage workers make ends meet, but it is also good for the economy. By providing workers with a living wage, we can reduce poverty, improve health outcomes, and stimulate economic growth. To summarize, the case for raising the minimum wage is clear and undeniable.

The Dilemma of Allocating Resources: Balancing Economic Growth and Environmental Sustainability

In today's world, the efficient allocation of resources has become a critical issue as we strive to achieve economic growth while also protecting the environment. On one hand, the need for economic development is paramount to improve the standard of living and provide job opportunities. On the other hand, overconsumption of resources can lead to severe environmental degradation and depletion of natural resources.

Critics of resource allocation argue that a focus on economic growth at the expense of the environment can have devastating consequences. For example, the rapid industrialization of many countries has led to increased pollution, deforestation, and depletion of vital resources like water and minerals. This, in turn, has resulted in a decline in biodiversity, soil degradation, and increased greenhouse gas emissions.

On the other hand, proponents argue that without economic growth, it is impossible to achieve sustainability. They argue that economic development provides the resources and funding necessary to implement effective environmental protection policies. Additionally, they argue that economic growth can help reduce poverty and improve the standard of living of people, leading to a healthier and more sustainable future.

In conclusion, the allocation of resources is a complex issue that requires a delicate balance between economic growth and environmental protection. The key to resolving this dilemma lies in finding a sustainable development path that ensures the efficient use of resources while also protecting the environment. This can be achieved through the implementation of policies that promote resource efficiency, renewable energy, and sustainable agriculture. By taking these steps, we can ensure that future generations have access to the resources they need to lead healthy and productive lives.

The Case for Abolishing Tests: A Critique of Traditional Assessment Methods

Assessment methods, such as tests and exams, have been used for decades to measure the knowledge and abilities of students. However, a growing body of research has called into question the validity and fairness of these traditional methods of assessment. On the one hand, supporters of tests argue that they provide an objective and standardized way of measuring student performance. On the other hand, critics argue that tests fail to accurately reflect the full range of a student's knowledge and skills, and can lead to unnecessary stress and anxiety. In this essay, I will examine both sides of the argument and make the case for why we should abolish tests as the sole means of assessment.

One of the main arguments in favour of tests is that they provide an objective and standardized way of measuring student performance. By using the same test for all students, teachers can compare the results and make fair and accurate assessments of their knowledge and abilities. Moreover, tests are considered to be an efficient and reliable way of assessing large numbers of students in a short amount of time.

However, on the contrary, tests have a number of serious drawbacks. For one, tests only measure a narrow range of a student's knowledge and abilities, and can be biased towards certain types of students, such as those who are good at taking tests or those who have been taught to memorize information rather than understand it. Additionally, tests can be stressful and anxiety-inducing for many students, which can lead to decreased motivation and reduced performance. Furthermore, tests can create a high-stakes environment where students are encouraged to cheat or engage in other unethical behaviours in order to improve their scores.

In conclusion, while tests may provide some benefits as a means of assessment, they also have serious drawbacks that make them an unreliable and unfair way of measuring student performance. Rather than relying solely on tests, we should move towards a more holistic approach to assessment that takes into account a student's full range of knowledge and skills. This may involve using a variety of assessment methods, such as projects, essays, and portfolios, which can provide a more accurate and complete picture of a student's abilities. By doing so, we can ensure that students are evaluated fairly and that their full potential is recognized and nurtured.

The Ethics of Eating Meat: A Debate on the Advantages and Disadvantages of Meat and Vegan Diets

The debate about whether to eat meat or follow a vegan diet has been a hot topic for many years. While some argue that meat is a necessary source of nutrients and protein, others argue that a plant-based diet is better for the environment and for our health. In this essay, I will explore both sides of the argument and come to a conclusion about the most ethical way to eat.

On the one hand, proponents of eating meat argue that it is a natural part of human evolution and that it provides essential nutrients and protein that cannot be found in plant-based foods. They argue that our ancestors have been eating meat for thousands of years, and that it is a natural part of our diet. Furthermore, they claim that meat is a good source of vitamins and minerals, such as iron and vitamin B12, that are essential for our health and well-being.

On the other hand, advocates of a vegan diet argue that eating meat is harmful to the environment and to our health. They argue that the production of meat contributes to deforestation, land degradation, and greenhouse gas emissions, and that a plant-based diet is better for the environment. Additionally, they claim that a vegan diet can help prevent chronic diseases, such as heart disease and cancer, and that it is more sustainable for the planet.

The bottom line is this. Both meat and vegan diets have advantages and disadvantages, and the decision to eat meat or follow a vegan diet is a personal one. While meat provides essential nutrients and protein, it is also associated with negative impacts on the environment and our health. On the other hand, a vegan diet can help reduce the impact on the environment, but it may not provide all the nutrients that our bodies need. Ultimately, the best approach is to find a balanced diet that meets our nutritional needs while also being mindful of the impact on the environment.

135

The Importance of Adequate Sleep: Arguing Against Sleeping Less than 8 Hours

It is a common misconception that one can function optimally on limited sleep. In fact, numerous studies have shown that consistently sleeping less than 8 hours per night has detrimental effects on both physical and mental health. On the one hand, not getting enough sleep can lead to decreased energy levels, increased stress and anxiety, decreased immune function, and even obesity. On the other hand, obtaining a sufficient amount of sleep has numerous benefits, such as improved memory and cognitive function, increased productivity, reduced stress, and better overall physical health.

The notion that sleeping less leads to increased productivity is a fallacy. Sure, it may allow for more waking hours, but the truth is that those extra hours are often spent in a drowsy and less productive state. The body requires rest in order to recharge, and without it, one is unable to perform at their full potential. In addition, lack of sleep has been linked to several serious health issues, including heart disease, depression, and stroke.

Furthermore, it is important to note that the amount of sleep required varies from person to person. Some people may function well on 6 hours of sleep, while others may need 9 or 10. It is crucial to listen to your body and give it the rest it needs in order to maintain good health.

All in all, sleeping less than 8 hours per night is not a sustainable solution to increasing productivity. Instead, it is a recipe for decreased performance and potential health issues. In order to lead a happy and healthy life, it is essential to prioritize adequate sleep. By doing so, one can reap the numerous benefits that come with a well-rested mind and body.

The Importance of Children Participating in Household Chores

In many households, the idea of children assisting with household chores is often met with resistance. Some argue that children should be free to enjoy their childhood, while others believe that chores are a responsibility that should only fall upon adults. However, the truth is that involving children in household chores can have numerous benefits for both the child and the household as a whole.

On the one hand, children who participate in household chores learn valuable life skills. Doing chores teaches children responsibility, organization, and the importance of contributing to a household. Children who help with household chores also develop a strong work ethic, which will serve them well in their future careers. By learning these skills at a young age, children are better equipped to handle the challenges of adulthood.

On the other hand, when children assist with household chores, they are also helping to ease the burden on their parents. In households where both parents work outside of the home, the workload can be overwhelming. Children who participate in household chores take some of the pressure off their parents, allowing them to focus on other tasks. This can lead to a more harmonious and stress-free home environment.

Moreover, involving children in household chores can also have a positive impact on their self-esteem. Children who feel valued and needed in their households are more likely to have high self-esteem. By helping with household chores, children feel like they are contributing to the household and making a difference. This can lead to a greater sense of purpose and fulfilment in their lives.

However, it is important to remember that children should not be overburdened with chores. The amount and type of chores children participate in should be appropriate for their age and abilities. For example, younger children may only be able to help with simple tasks, such as setting the table, while older children may be able to handle more complex tasks, such as cleaning the bathroom.

In a nutshell, involving children in household chores is a beneficial practice for both children and parents. By learning valuable life skills, easing the burden on parents, and positively impacting children's self-esteem, participating in household chores can help children develop into well-rounded and responsible adults.

The Pros and Cons of Solo Learning versus Learning with a Teacher

Studying with a teacher or studying alone: which is the better option for success in education? This has been a long-standing debate among students and educators alike, with arguments for both sides. While some believe that studying with a teacher provides accountability and structure, others argue that the ability to learn at one's own pace and in a comfortable environment is what leads to the best educational outcomes.

On the one hand, studying with a teacher has its advantages. Firstly, it provides accountability. When studying with a teacher, students are held responsible for their progress, and they are less likely to neglect their studies. A teacher can also act as a mentor, guiding students through difficult subjects and helping them to set achievable goals. Additionally, studying with a teacher can provide students with structure and discipline. This can be particularly useful for students who struggle with time management or motivation. In a classroom setting, students are expected to arrive on time, pay attention, and participate in class activities, which can help them to develop strong study habits.

On the other hand, studying alone has its benefits as well. Firstly, students have the ability to learn at their own pace. When studying alone, students can take as much time as they need to understand a concept, without feeling pressured to keep up with the pace of the class. This can help students to feel more confident in their abilities, as well as reducing feelings of frustration or burnout. Secondly, studying alone allows students to create a comfortable and distraction-free environment, which can be beneficial for concentration and memory retention. Students can choose the environment that works best for them, whether it's a quiet library, a bustling coffee shop, or even their own bedroom. Finally, studying alone can help students to develop their own learning style and strategy, which can be crucial for success in higher education.

In conclusion, whether studying with a teacher or studying alone is the better option depends on the individual student and their unique needs and preferences. For some students, studying with a teacher provides the structure and accountability they need to succeed, while others may benefit more from the freedom and flexibility of studying alone. Ultimately, the key to success in education is finding what works best for you, and being willing to experiment with different approaches until you find what works best.

Family vs Friends: Who Offers the Strongest Support?

In today's society, people often turn to both family and friends when they need support. But which of the two groups offers the strongest support? Some may argue that family provides the strongest support because they are blood-related and share a deep emotional connection, while others may argue that friends offer stronger support because they are chosen by the individual and are often more understanding and accepting. In this essay, I will examine the strengths and weaknesses of both family and friends as sources of support.

On the one hand, family provides a strong support system because of the shared history and emotional connection. Family members have known each other for a lifetime and have shared many experiences together. As a result, family members are often more understanding and forgiving of one another. This strong emotional connection makes family a great source of support, particularly during difficult times.

On the other hand, friends offer a unique type of support that is not always found in family relationships. Friends are individuals who have been chosen by the individual and are often more understanding and accepting of the individual's quirks and quirks. Unlike family members, who are often bound by tradition and expectation, friends are free to be themselves and offer support without judgment. This makes friends a great source of support for individuals who may not feel comfortable turning to their family for help.

As a conclusion, both family and friends play important roles in offering support, and the choice of which group offers the strongest support depends on the individual and their needs. For those who need a strong emotional connection, family is often the best choice. For those who need acceptance and understanding, friends are often a better option. Ultimately, both family and friends can offer support, and it is up to the individual to decide which group is best suited to meet their needs.

Family vs Friends: Which Provides More Support and Satisfaction in Life?

In today's world, people are often faced with the dilemma of choosing between their family and their friends. On the one hand, family members are considered to be the closest and most dependable people in our lives. They are the ones who are there for us from the beginning of our lives, providing us with unconditional love and support. On the other hand, friends are the individuals whom we choose to surround ourselves with and form close bonds with through shared experiences and common interests. Both family and friends play a vital role in our lives, but the question remains, which one provides us with more support and satisfaction in life?

On one hand, family is considered to be the backbone of our lives. They provide us with the emotional, financial, and physical support that we need to survive and thrive. Family members are often the first people we turn to in times of crisis, and they are there to offer us their unwavering support, whether it be through a simple listening ear or practical assistance. Furthermore, families also play a crucial role in shaping our values and beliefs, as well as our overall character.

However, on the other hand, friends also provide us with unique benefits that are different from those provided by family members. Friends offer us the opportunity to explore new interests and experiences, and to engage in activities that we may not be able to do with our family members. They also provide us with the opportunity to have open and honest conversations, as well as to receive constructive criticism from those who care about us.

In terms of support, both family and friends play a vital role in our lives. Family members provide us with the love and care that we need to thrive, while friends provide us with the social interaction and companionship that we need to maintain our mental and emotional well-being. Ultimately, both family and friends play a crucial role in our lives, and it is up to each individual to determine which group provides them with the most support and satisfaction.

To wrap things up, the choice between family and friends is a complex one that requires careful consideration of the different benefits and drawbacks of each group. While family members provide us with the stability and support that we need to survive, friends provide us with the experiences and companionship that we need to thrive. In the end, the key to happiness and satisfaction in life is to find a balance between both family and friends, and to make sure that we are surrounded by people who love and support us, no matter what.

The Eternal Dilemma: Staying Married or Opting for Divorce

Marriage is a lifelong commitment, but for some couples, the bond that once brought them together can become strained and eventually lead to divorce. On the one hand, some argue that staying married is a better option as it offers stability and security to the individuals involved, as well as to any children involved in the marriage. On the other hand, proponents of divorce argue that it is sometimes necessary to end a toxic or unhappy marriage in order to allow both partners to pursue their individual happiness.

One of the main arguments for staying married is that it offers stability and security to the individuals involved. When people are married, they have the assurance of a committed partner who is there for them through thick and thin. This stability is particularly important for those with children, as children thrive in a stable and secure environment. Moreover, staying married also provides financial benefits, such as tax breaks and shared assets, that can make it easier for individuals to manage their finances and provide for their family.

On the contrary, those who support divorce argue that it is sometimes necessary to end a toxic or unhappy marriage. When a marriage becomes toxic, it can be damaging to the individuals involved, as well as to any children involved in the marriage. A toxic or unhappy marriage can lead to emotional distress, depression, and even physical health problems, which can impact the quality of life for everyone involved. Divorce can also be the best option for individuals who are no longer compatible or who have grown apart, as it allows them to pursue their individual happiness and live their lives on their own terms.

Despite the arguments in favour of staying married, there are also some compelling arguments in favour of divorce. For example, research has shown that people who are divorced are generally happier and more fulfilled than those who remain in unhappy marriages. Additionally, divorce can also provide individuals with a fresh start and the opportunity to rebuild their lives in a more positive and fulfilling way.

Ultimately, the decision to stay married or opt for divorce is a personal one that must be made by each individual couple. While staying married offers stability and security, divorce can provide a chance for individuals to pursue their individual happiness and start anew. Both options have their advantages and disadvantages, and the decision must be based on a careful consideration of the specific circumstances of each case. Whether one chooses to stay married or divorce, the important thing is to prioritize the well-being of all individuals involved, including any children, and to work towards a solution that is in their best interests.

The Impact of Video Games on Children: To Play or Not to Play?

In recent years, video games have become increasingly popular among children, with the rise of technology and accessible gaming devices. While some argue that video games can have a positive impact on children, such as improving hand-eye coordination, problem-solving skills, and creativity, others believe that video games can have negative effects on children, such as promoting violence and addiction. This argumentative essay will examine the pros and cons of allowing children to play video games and come to a conclusion about whether or not it is a good idea.

On the one hand, video games can provide numerous benefits for children. For example, playing video games can improve hand-eye coordination, which can lead to better fine motor skills. Additionally, video games often require players to solve puzzles and complete tasks, which can help develop problem-solving skills and critical thinking. Furthermore, video games can also stimulate creativity, as children are able to imagine new worlds and storylines.

On the other hand, video games can also have negative effects on children. One of the biggest concerns is the potential for violence, as some video games feature violent themes and actions. This can lead to desensitization to violence and aggressive behaviour. Furthermore, video games can also be addictive, with children spending excessive amounts of time playing and neglecting other important activities, such as schoolwork and physical exercise.

In order to ensure that children reap the benefits of video games while minimizing the negative effects, it is important to establish boundaries and guidelines. For example, parents should limit the amount of time that their children spend playing video games, and ensure that they are playing age-appropriate games. Additionally, parents should also encourage children to engage in a variety of other activities, such as sports, arts, and reading, to promote a well-rounded lifestyle.

In conclusion, video games can have both positive and negative impacts on children. While playing video games can improve hand-eye coordination, problem-solving skills, and creativity, it can also lead to violence, addiction, and neglect of other important activities. To ensure that children are able to enjoy the benefits of video games while avoiding the drawbacks, it is crucial for parents to establish clear boundaries and guidelines. Ultimately, whether or not children should play video games is a complex issue, and the answer will vary from child to child. However, with the right approach, video games can be a valuable tool for children's development and enjoyment.

The Great Debate: Books vs eBooks: Which is the Better Option for Reading?

Books and eBooks have been the subject of much debate in recent years, as technology continues to advance and change the way we live our lives. On one hand, traditional books are beloved for their physicality and the sensory experience they provide. They offer a timeless charm that cannot be replicated by digital devices, and they are often treasured as much for their aesthetic value as they are for their content. On the other hand, eBooks are becoming increasingly popular, particularly among younger generations, due to their portability, accessibility, and versatility.

One of the main advantages of books is the tactile experience they provide. Many people enjoy the sensation of turning pages and holding a physical book in their hands, and they find that this contributes to a deeper connection with the story or information they are reading. Furthermore, books often have a timeless quality that eBooks lack. While digital devices and software are constantly changing, books are relatively unchanged since their invention, and many people appreciate their unchanging nature.

However, there are also many benefits to using eBooks. One of the main advantages of eBooks is their portability. They can be stored on a single device, such as a tablet or e-reader, and this allows people to carry hundreds or even thousands of books with them wherever they go. This is particularly useful for travellers, who may not want to carry multiple physical books with them on a trip. In addition, eBooks are often cheaper than physical books, and they can be purchased and downloaded instantly, making them more convenient and accessible for many people.

Another advantage of eBooks is their versatility. They can be adjusted to suit the needs of individual users, with options for changing the font size, style, and background colour, making them easier to read for those with visual impairments. They also offer interactive features, such as hyperlinks, that can enhance the reading experience.

On the whole, books and eBooks each have their own unique advantages and disadvantages, and the choice between them will depend on individual preferences and needs. While books provide a timeless and tactile experience, eBooks offer portability, accessibility, and versatility. Ultimately, the choice between books and eBooks is a personal one, and there is no right or wrong answer.

The Benefits of Doing What You Don't Enjoy: An Argument for Embracing the Unpleasant

Many people believe that they should only do things that they enjoy and find pleasurable. However, this notion can be limiting, as it prevents individuals from growing and developing new skills. On the other hand, engaging in activities that one does not enjoy can lead to numerous benefits, including personal growth, character development, and improved resilience. In this essay, we will examine the arguments for why people should sometimes do things they do not enjoy.

One of the primary benefits of doing things that you do not enjoy is personal growth and development. Engaging in activities that are outside of your comfort zone can help you develop new skills, such as patience, perseverance, and problem-solving. These skills are essential for success in both personal and professional life and can help individuals become more well-rounded and confident. For example, if someone is not naturally athletic, they may push themselves to take up a sport that they find challenging. Through consistent practice and dedication, they will likely improve their athletic abilities, thereby enhancing their overall physical fitness and well-being.

Another benefit of doing things that you do not enjoy is character development. Engaging in activities that push you out of your comfort zone can help you build resilience, determination, and a strong work ethic. These qualities are essential for success in life and are developed through overcoming challenges and persevering in the face of adversity. For instance, if someone finds public speaking to be extremely nerve-wracking, they may decide to take a public speaking course to build their confidence. Through consistent practice and determination, they will likely become a more confident and effective public speaker.

Finally, doing things that you do not enjoy can also help improve your resilience. Resilience is the ability to bounce back from setbacks, challenges, and difficulties. Engaging in activities that are difficult or unpleasant can help individuals develop a stronger sense of resilience, as they will be better equipped to handle challenges that they may face in the future. For example, if someone is not naturally organized, they may decide to take a course on time management and organization. By tackling this difficult task, they will likely become more organized and resilient, enabling them to handle the many challenges that life throws their way.

When all things considered, while it may be tempting to only do things that one finds enjoyable, engaging in activities that are outside of one's comfort zone can lead to numerous benefits, including personal growth, character development, and improved resilience. So, the next time you find yourself faced with a task that you do not enjoy, consider embracing the challenge and pushing yourself out of your comfort zone. You never know what you may learn or the growth you may experience as a result.

Should College Education Be Free?

In recent years, the cost of college education has skyrocketed, leaving many students and families burdened with debt that takes years to pay off. This has led to a debate on whether college education should be free. While some argue that free college education is essential for ensuring access to higher education, others believe that it would be a burden on taxpayers. In my opinion, college education should be free for all students.

Firstly, college education is an essential tool for social mobility and economic growth. Access to higher education should not be limited to those who can afford it. By making college education free, the government can provide opportunities to students from low-income families, who might not be able to afford college education otherwise. This would ensure that students are not denied the chance to pursue higher education based on their financial status.

Secondly, providing free college education can lead to a more educated workforce. With a highly educated workforce, the country can benefit from a higher GDP, increased productivity, and innovation. This, in turn, can lead to a more prosperous society. Additionally, by providing free college education, the government can ensure that students are not burdened with debt, which can affect their ability to start a family or buy a home.

However, opponents argue that providing free college education would be a burden on taxpayers. They argue that the government would have to increase taxes to fund free college education. However, studies have shown that providing free college education would result in long-term benefits, such as a more educated workforce and a higher GDP, which would generate additional revenue for the government.

Considering everything, college education should be free for all students. Access to higher education is essential for social mobility and economic growth, and making college education free would ensure that students from all economic backgrounds have equal opportunities to pursue higher education. While opponents argue that providing free college education would be a burden on taxpayers, the long-term benefits of a more educated workforce and a higher GDP would generate additional revenue for the government.

The Urgency of Addressing Climate Change

Climate change is a pressing issue that has far-reaching consequences for the planet and all its inhabitants. The scientific community has been warning about the effects of global warming for decades, and the evidence of its impact is clear. The debate now is how to respond to this challenge. While some may argue that climate change is an overblown concern, it is essential to recognize that the problem is real and that action is necessary to address it.

One of the main arguments against climate change action is that it will be too costly for economies and that the costs outweigh the benefits. While it is true that there will be upfront costs to reducing carbon emissions and transitioning to renewable energy, the long-term costs of doing nothing are far greater. Climate change is already resulting in more frequent and severe weather events, sea level rise, and melting glaciers, among other impacts. The cost of inaction will only continue to grow, resulting in far-reaching ecological and economic consequences.

Another argument against climate change action is that individual actions are not enough to make a difference. While it is true that individual actions alone may not be sufficient to address climate change, they are still an essential part of the solution. Small changes in individual behaviour can add up to significant reductions in carbon emissions. Governments, businesses, and individuals all have a role to play in reducing their carbon footprint and transitioning to more sustainable practices.

The most significant argument for taking action on climate change is that the consequences of inaction are simply too severe to ignore. The current trajectory of carbon emissions and temperature rise is projected to cause irreversible damage to the planet, resulting in a range of impacts, including mass extinction of species, widespread food and water shortages, and more frequent and severe weather events. The only way to prevent this outcome is to take immediate and comprehensive action to reduce carbon emissions and transition to renewable energy sources.

Generally speaking, climate change is an urgent and pressing issue that requires immediate action. The cost of inaction is too great to ignore, and while there may be challenges to addressing this problem, they are far outweighed by the potential consequences of doing nothing. Individuals, governments, and businesses all have a role to play in reducing their carbon footprint and transitioning to more sustainable practices. It is time to take responsibility for our impact on the planet and take the necessary action to address climate change.

Should Abortion be Banned?

Abortion is one of the most controversial topics of our time. It has been debated for many years, and people are still divided on the issue. Some people believe that abortion should be banned, while others believe that it should remain legal. In this essay, I will argue that abortion should not be banned.

Firstly, women should have the right to make their own decisions about their bodies. The decision to have an abortion is a personal one, and it should not be influenced by laws or regulations. Women should be able to choose what is best for them and their families. Banning abortion takes away this freedom of choice.

Secondly, banning abortion will not stop it from happening. It will only drive women to seek unsafe and illegal procedures, which can have serious consequences. Studies have shown that when abortion is illegal, the number of unsafe abortions and maternal deaths increase. This is because women are forced to resort to dangerous methods to terminate their pregnancies.

Thirdly, banning abortion is a violation of human rights. Women have the right to access safe and legal abortion services, which is recognized by international human rights treaties. Denying women this right is a violation of their basic human rights.

On the other hand, those who argue for the ban of abortion believe that it is immoral and goes against religious and moral values. They believe that life begins at conception, and therefore, abortion is equivalent to murder.

However, it is important to recognize that not everyone shares the same religious or moral beliefs. It is not appropriate to impose one's beliefs on others through laws and regulations.

In conclusion, banning abortion is not the solution to reducing the number of abortions. It will only lead to unsafe and illegal procedures, and it is a violation of women's basic human rights. Women should have the right to make their own decisions about their bodies, and access to safe and legal abortion services should be protected.

The Debate on Granting Residency to Illegal Immigrants

Illegal immigration has been a contentious issue for years, and one of the most controversial aspects of this debate is whether illegal immigrants should be granted residency. On one hand, some argue that granting residency would provide them with better access to healthcare, education, and employment opportunities. On the other hand, opponents of residency for illegal immigrants argue that it would reward law-breaking behaviour and create an incentive for more people to enter the country illegally.

Those in favour of granting residency to illegal immigrants argue that it is the moral and ethical thing to do. Many of these individuals have been living and working in the United States for years, and have established lives and families here. By granting them residency, they would be able to obtain better-paying jobs, access higher education, and have better access to healthcare. Moreover, these individuals contribute to society by paying taxes, and in many cases, they have no criminal record.

Opponents, on the other hand, argue that granting residency would create a dangerous precedent. If the government were to provide amnesty to those who have broken the law by entering the country illegally, it would encourage others to do the same. Furthermore, it would create an unfair advantage for those who have entered the country illegally over those who have gone through the legal process of obtaining residency or citizenship. The government should prioritize those who have followed the rules, and grant residency only to those who have entered the country legally.

Moreover, granting residency to illegal immigrants can have negative economic impacts. It could result in higher taxes for citizens, and a burden on social welfare programs. It could also increase competition for jobs, causing wages to decrease for citizens and legal residents. Furthermore, it would send the message that the government is willing to reward those who break the law, which could undermine the integrity of the legal system.

In conclusion, the debate over granting residency to illegal immigrants is complex and multifaceted. While some argue that it is the humane and ethical thing to do, others argue that it could have negative economic and social impacts. It is essential to consider both sides of the argument and weigh the potential consequences before making any decisions. Ultimately, the government should prioritize the safety and well-being of its citizens and legal residents, while also upholding the values of fairness and justice.

The Pros and Cons of Socialism and Capitalism

In today's society, there are two dominant economic systems: socialism and capitalism. While both have their advantages and disadvantages, there has always been a debate on which is better. Socialism is based on the idea that wealth and resources should be shared equally among the citizens, while capitalism is based on the idea that the government should not interfere in the economy, and individuals should be free to create and sell products as they see fit. In this essay, we will examine the pros and cons of both socialism and capitalism.

One of the biggest advantages of socialism is that it reduces economic inequality. In a socialist system, everyone has equal access to healthcare, education, and other basic necessities. The government is responsible for ensuring that everyone has the same opportunities, regardless of their socioeconomic status. Additionally, under socialism, there is less poverty, as the government provides assistance to those who need it.

On the other hand, one of the main drawbacks of socialism is that it can stifle innovation and entrepreneurship. In a socialist system, the government owns and controls most businesses, which can limit competition and reduce the incentives for people to create new products and services. As a result, there may be less economic growth under socialism, and fewer opportunities for individuals to create wealth.

Capitalism, on the other hand, is based on the idea of individual freedom and the pursuit of self-interest. One of the main advantages of capitalism is that it promotes innovation and entrepreneurship. Since individuals are free to create and sell products as they see fit, there is more competition, which drives innovation and leads to economic growth. Additionally, capitalism provides incentives for individuals to work hard and create wealth, which can improve the overall standard of living.

However, capitalism also has its disadvantages. One of the main drawbacks of capitalism is that it can lead to economic inequality. In a capitalist system, those who have more money and resources are often able to accumulate even more wealth, while those who have less may struggle to make ends meet. Additionally, capitalism can sometimes lead to monopolies and unfair business practices, as companies try to gain a competitive advantage over others.

In short, both socialism and capitalism have their advantages and disadvantages. Socialism can reduce economic inequality and poverty, but may stifle innovation and entrepreneurship. Capitalism can promote innovation and economic growth, but may lead to economic inequality and unfair business practices. Ultimately, the choice between socialism and capitalism depends on what values society wants to prioritize: equality or freedom.

Should Smoking Be Made Illegal?

Smoking has been a controversial topic for decades. While some people argue that smoking is a personal choice and should not be banned, others believe that smoking should be made illegal because of the health risks associated with it. In this essay, we will explore the reasons why smoking should be banned and why it is important for society as a whole.

Firstly, smoking has been proven to cause a wide range of health problems, including lung cancer, heart disease, and respiratory problems. The chemicals in cigarettes are toxic and can cause damage to the body, even in small amounts. Second-hand smoke can also be harmful to those around the smoker, including children and pregnant women. By making smoking illegal, we could potentially save countless lives and prevent unnecessary suffering.

Secondly, smoking is a drain on the economy. Smoking-related illnesses and diseases cost billions of dollars in healthcare costs every year. In addition, smoking is a leading cause of preventable deaths, which means that people are dying prematurely, and families are left without loved ones. By making smoking illegal, we could reduce the economic burden of smoking on society and redirect those resources towards more productive areas.

Finally, smoking is harmful to the environment. Cigarette butts are the most common form of litter and take years to decompose. The production and transportation of cigarettes also contribute to air pollution and deforestation. By making smoking illegal, we could reduce the environmental impact of smoking and promote a healthier planet.

On the other hand, some people argue that smoking is a personal choice and that making it illegal would infringe on people's rights. They also argue that prohibition has not worked in the past, and that people would find ways to smoke regardless of whether it is legal or not.

However, we must consider the larger societal impact of smoking. Smoking affects not only the smoker but also the people around them, the economy, and the environment. It is our responsibility as a society to protect the health and wellbeing of all individuals, and making smoking illegal would be a step in the right direction.

In conclusion, smoking should be made illegal for the sake of public health, the economy, and the environment. While some may argue that it is a personal choice, the larger societal impact of smoking cannot be ignored. By banning smoking, we could save lives, reduce healthcare costs, and create a healthier planet for future generations.

The Importance of Achieving Gender Equality

Gender equality has been an ongoing issue for centuries, and despite significant progress being made in recent years, there is still a long way to go. Women have fought hard to gain equal rights in various aspects of life, including education, the workplace, and politics. However, there are still many inequalities and biases that need to be addressed, and it is crucial that we continue to strive for gender equality. In this essay, I will argue that achieving gender equality is important for a fair and just society.

One of the main reasons why gender equality is crucial is that it is a fundamental human right. Both men and women have the right to be treated equally, and this should be reflected in all areas of life, including education, employment, and politics. Denying women these rights is a form of discrimination that is unfair and unjust.

Achieving gender equality is also essential for the economic growth and development of a country. When women are given the same opportunities and rights as men, they can contribute to the workforce and the economy. Research has shown that gender equality can lead to increased productivity, higher GDP, and reduced poverty. Additionally, gender diversity in the workplace can bring different perspectives and ideas, leading to innovation and growth.

Furthermore, gender equality is essential for a safe and peaceful society. When women are empowered and given equal rights, they are less likely to experience violence, discrimination, and abuse. Gender-based violence is a widespread problem that affects millions of women around the world, and achieving gender equality is crucial in reducing this violence.

However, some argue that men and women are inherently different and therefore cannot be equal. While there may be some biological differences between men and women, these differences do not justify discrimination and inequality. In fact, many of the differences that exist between men and women are due to socialization and cultural expectations, rather than biology.

In conclusion, achieving gender equality is important for a fair, just, and prosperous society. It is a fundamental human right and essential for economic growth, peaceful and safe societies, and reducing gender-based violence. While progress has been made in recent years, there is still a long way to go, and we must continue to work towards achieving gender equality.

The Pros and Cons of a Fully Cashless World

In today's digital age, the concept of a cashless society is becoming more common. With the rise of digital payment options and mobile wallets, some have argued that a fully cashless world could offer many benefits, including convenience, security, and increased financial transparency. However, others believe that a cashless society could have negative consequences, such as exclusion of certain populations, increased surveillance, and vulnerability to cyber-attacks. In this essay, I will explore the pros and cons of a fully cashless world.

One of the main benefits of a cashless society is the convenience it offers. With digital payment options and mobile wallets, people no longer have to carry cash or worry about losing it. Digital payments can also be made quickly and easily, making transactions more efficient. Additionally, a cashless society could reduce the costs associated with printing, storing, and transporting physical currency.

Another advantage of a cashless society is increased financial transparency. Digital payments leave a clear record of transactions, which could help combat money laundering and tax evasion. This transparency could also make it easier for governments to track and monitor financial transactions, which could help reduce corruption and crime.

However, there are also several drawbacks to a fully cashless world. One of the biggest concerns is exclusion of certain populations, such as those without access to digital payment options. This could disproportionately impact low-income individuals, the elderly, and those living in rural areas where internet and digital infrastructure may be limited.

Another potential downside is increased surveillance. Digital payment systems are inherently traceable, which could lead to greater surveillance and monitoring of financial transactions by governments or corporations. This could raise concerns about privacy and civil liberties.

Finally, a cashless society may also be vulnerable to cyber-attacks. If all financial transactions are conducted digitally, a successful cyber-attack could cause widespread financial chaos and could even destabilize the entire economy.

In conclusion, while a fully cashless world may offer certain benefits such as convenience, increased financial transparency, and reduced costs, it also raises concerns about exclusion, increased surveillance, and vulnerability to cyber-attacks. As we move towards a more digitized world, it is important to consider the potential consequences of a cashless society and strive to create systems that are inclusive, secure, and protect individual rights and liberties.

Video Games as a Sport

Video games have become increasingly popular in recent years, and the rise of competitive gaming, or "esports," has led some to argue that video games should be considered a sport. While there are certainly similarities between traditional sports and esports, there are also some key differences that make it difficult to argue that video games should be considered a sport.

On the one hand, there are some compelling arguments in favour of recognizing esports as a legitimate sport. Many esports require the same level of skill, strategy, and teamwork as traditional sports, and top esports players can earn millions of dollars in prize money. Additionally, esports are played in organized leagues and tournaments, with rules and regulations designed to ensure fair competition.

On the other hand, there are some key differences between video games and traditional sports that make it difficult to argue that video games should be considered a sport. For one thing, video games are typically played on a screen, which is a much different physical experience than playing a sport in the physical world. Additionally, many video games are not physically demanding, which is a key characteristic of traditional sports. While some esports, such as virtual reality games, may require physical movement, the vast majority of esports do not.

Another argument against recognizing esports as a sport is that it could lead to a devaluation of what we traditionally think of as sports. This is not to say that esports are less valid or less challenging than traditional sports, but rather that they are fundamentally different experiences. By trying to force video games into the same category as traditional sports, we may be overlooking the unique qualities and strengths of each.

Ultimately, while there are compelling arguments on both sides of the debate, it seems unlikely that video games will ever fully be accepted as a sport. However, this doesn't mean that esports can't be taken seriously and valued for their own unique strengths and qualities. As the popularity of esports continues to grow, it's important to recognize their value and give them the recognition and respect that they deserve.

The Challenges Faced by the Younger Generation Compared to Their Parents

In recent years, there has been a growing concern that the younger generation is facing more challenges than their parents once did. Some people argue that the younger generation is not as resilient and hardworking as their parents, while others believe that the challenges faced by the younger generation are unique and require different strategies to overcome. This essay will explore the challenges faced by the younger generation and how they compare to those faced by their parents.

One of the most significant challenges facing the younger generation is the economy. The younger generation is struggling with lower wages, higher costs of living, and more significant debt than their parents once did. The job market is more competitive, and young people are facing an uncertain future with little job security. Additionally, younger people are dealing with rising levels of student debt, making it more difficult to save for a home or other significant investments.

Another challenge facing the younger generation is the impact of technology on their lives. While technology has made life more convenient and connected, it has also created new problems. Young people are experiencing more stress and anxiety due to social media, and there is a growing concern about the impact of technology on mental health. Additionally, many young people are struggling to find a balance between work and leisure time, as technology has made it easier to work from home and stay connected to the office 24/7.

Finally, the younger generation is facing a world that is more diverse and interconnected than ever before. While this can be a positive thing, it also presents unique challenges. Young people are exposed to more diverse opinions and cultures, which can be challenging to navigate.

Additionally, there is a growing concern about the impact of climate change, and young people are taking on the burden of fighting for a more sustainable future.

In brief, the challenges faced by the younger generation are unique and complex. While their parents faced their own challenges, the younger generation is dealing with an economy that is more uncertain, the impact of technology on their lives, and a more interconnected and diverse world. It is essential to recognize these challenges and work to find solutions that support the younger generation in achieving their goals and aspirations.

Should Student Grades Be Publicly Disclosed?

In today's world, education plays an essential role in building a better future. Grades are one of the main metrics used to evaluate a student's academic performance. However, the debate on whether student grades should be publicly disclosed or not has been a subject of discussion for some time. While some argue that public disclosure of student grades can lead to increased competition and motivation, others believe it can lead to negative consequences such as stress and anxiety. In this essay, I will argue that student grades should not be publicly disclosed.

Firstly, public disclosure of grades can create unnecessary stress and anxiety for students. Students already face a lot of pressure to succeed, and public disclosure of their grades can add an additional layer of stress. It can also lead to a fear of failure, which can be detrimental to a student's mental health. If students feel like their grades are constantly being scrutinized and evaluated by their peers, they may be more likely to engage in academic dishonesty, such as cheating or plagiarism, to maintain their grades.

Secondly, public disclosure of grades can create unhealthy competition and discourage collaboration among students. When students are encouraged to compete with each other, they may lose sight of the importance of working together and helping each other to learn. This can lead to a toxic academic environment where students are more focused on outdoing their peers rather than working together to achieve a common goal. This kind of environment is not conducive to effective learning and may even lead to lower academic performance in the long run.

Furthermore, public disclosure of grades can have a negative impact on student-teacher relationships. If grades are publicly disclosed, it can create an unhealthy power dynamic between students and teachers. Teachers may feel more pressure to evaluate students strictly, which can create tension and even resentment between students and teachers. Students may also feel that their relationship with their teacher is based solely on their grades, rather than their potential to learn and grow.

In conclusion, while public disclosure of student grades may seem like a way to increase competition and motivation, it can ultimately have negative consequences for students' mental health, collaboration, and relationships with their teachers. Instead, we should focus on creating an environment where students are encouraged to learn and grow, rather than to compete with their peers. By doing so, we can help create a healthier and more supportive academic environment for all students.

Should You Leave or Stay at a Job That Makes You Unhappy?

In today's fast-paced world, it's not uncommon to feel stressed and unhappy with your job. The 9-5 grind can be a gruelling experience, but what happens when the job that's paying your bills is making you miserable? Should you tough it out and stay in the position or should you leave and find a new job? This is a tough decision that many people face, and the answer is not always straightforward.

On one hand, leaving a job can be a risky move, especially if you don't have another job lined up. You may have bills to pay, a family to support, and responsibilities that require a steady income. You may also worry about how your decision to leave will be perceived by your friends, family, and colleagues. Quitting your job without a backup plan can also lead to feelings of regret and self-doubt if things don't work out as planned.

On the other hand, staying at a job that makes you unhappy can take a serious toll on your mental health and well-being. It can lead to stress, burnout, and a general feeling of unhappiness that can spill over into other areas of your life. You may also feel stuck in a dead-end job with no room for growth or development. In some cases, staying in a job that's making you unhappy can be detrimental to your career growth and financial stability in the long run.

So, what should you do? Ultimately, the decision to stay or leave a job that makes you unhappy is a personal one that should be made after careful consideration. It's important to weigh the pros and cons of both options and assess your personal circumstances before making a decision. You should also think about what you really want in life and what makes you happy. If you're not sure, taking some time to reflect on your goals and priorities can help you make a more informed decision.

At the end of the day, the decision to leave or stay at a job that makes you unhappy is a difficult one, but nevertheless, it's up to you to make the right choice for your personal and professional growth. You should consider your financial obligations, career goals, and personal happiness when making the decision, and remember that sometimes taking a risk and stepping outside your comfort zone can lead to greater rewards in the long run.

Working for Yourself or Working for Others: The Pros and Cons

In today's world, there are many different career paths to choose from. One of the biggest decisions you may face is whether to work for yourself or for someone else. Both have their pros and cons, and it ultimately depends on your personality, preferences, and goals. In this essay, we will explore the advantages and disadvantages of working for yourself versus working for others.

One of the biggest advantages of working for yourself is the freedom and control it provides. You have the ability to make your own decisions and work on your own terms. You can choose your own hours, set your own goals, and pursue your own interests. This level of autonomy can be incredibly empowering and fulfilling.

However, this level of freedom can also be overwhelming and stressful. When you work for yourself, you are responsible for everything - from finding clients to managing your finances. You have to be self-motivated, disciplined, and willing to take risks. You may also have to work long hours and face uncertain income.

On the other hand, working for others can provide stability, structure, and support. You have a clear set of responsibilities, a regular pay check, and access to benefits like health insurance and retirement plans. You also have the opportunity to learn from others and work in a team environment.

However, working for others can also be limiting and frustrating. You may have less control over your work and your schedule, and your ideas and creativity may be stifled by corporate rules and regulations. You may also feel undervalued and unappreciated by your employer.

In a nutshell, whether you should work for yourself or for others ultimately depends on your own preferences, goals, and priorities. Working for yourself can provide a level of autonomy and fulfilment that is hard to find elsewhere, but it can also be stressful and challenging. Working for others can provide stability and support, but it can also be limiting and frustrating. The key is to weigh the pros and cons and choose the path that is best for you.

The Pros and Cons of Comparing Yourself with Others

Comparing yourself with others can be a double-edged sword. On one hand, it can motivate you to work harder and strive for success. On the other hand, it can lead to feelings of inadequacy and cause unnecessary stress. Therefore, it is important to weigh the pros and cons before deciding whether to compare yourself with others.

One of the advantages of comparing yourself with others is that it can inspire you to achieve more. Seeing others achieve their goals can motivate you to work harder and set higher standards for yourself. For example, if you have a colleague who is very successful in your field, seeing their success can inspire you to work harder and strive for similar achievements.

Another advantage of comparison is that it can help you identify areas for improvement. Seeing where others excel can highlight areas in which you could improve, allowing you to set goals and work towards improving your own skills and abilities.

However, comparing yourself with others can also have negative effects on your mental health. Constantly comparing yourself to others can lead to feelings of inadequacy and low self-esteem. You may begin to feel like you are not good enough, or that your achievements are not significant compared to others.

In addition, comparison can lead to unnecessary stress and anxiety. If you are constantly worried about how you measure up to others, you may find it difficult to focus on your own goals and achievements. This can lead to feelings of burnout and fatigue, which can ultimately impact your performance and success.

As a conclusion, comparing yourself with others can have both positive and negative effects. While it can be motivating and help identify areas for improvement, it can also lead to feelings of inadequacy and unnecessary stress. The key is to strike a balance between being inspired by others' successes while still focusing on your own goals and achievements. It is important to remember that everyone's journey is different, and that success is not a one-size-fits-all concept. Ultimately, it is up to each individual to decide whether comparison is a helpful or harmful practice.

The Pros and Cons of Paying Kids for Good Grades

In recent years, there has been a growing trend among parents to pay their children for getting good grades in school. While some argue that it is a good way to motivate children to do better in school, others believe that it sends the wrong message and can have negative consequences. In this essay, we will explore the pros and cons of paying kids for good grades.

One of the main arguments in favour of paying kids for good grades is that it can be a strong motivator. By offering a financial reward for doing well in school, children may be more inclined to put in the effort to get good grades. This could lead to better academic performance, which in turn can improve their chances of getting into a good college or finding a good job in the future.

On the other hand, some argue that paying kids for good grades can send the wrong message. It can create a situation where children view learning as something that they only do for financial gain, rather than for its own intrinsic value. This could lead to a situation where they become less interested in learning and may even cheat or cut corners in order to get good grades and earn more money.

Another concern with paying kids for good grades is that it could create unnecessary stress and pressure. Children may feel like they have to perform at a high level in order to earn money, which can be a lot of pressure for a young person. This could lead to increased anxiety and stress, which could have negative effects on their mental health.

In addition to these potential negative consequences, there is also a concern that paying kids for good grades could be unfair to those who are not able to earn good grades for various reasons. For example, children with learning disabilities or other challenges may struggle to get good grades even with extra effort, and they may feel like they are being unfairly penalized for something that is out of their control.

In conclusion, the decision to pay kids for good grades is a complex issue with both pros and cons. While it can be a strong motivator for some children, it can also send the wrong message and create unnecessary stress and pressure. Ultimately, parents must weigh the potential benefits against the potential risks and make a decision that is best for their individual child.

The Relevance of Tertiary Education in Today's Society

In the current era, there is an ongoing debate about the relevance and necessity of tertiary education. While some believe that tertiary education is a critical component of career success, others argue that its cost and time commitment make it less valuable than alternatives.

Proponents of tertiary education argue that it is essential for career success. They suggest that it provides individuals with the necessary knowledge and skills to excel in their chosen fields, and gives them a competitive edge in the job market. They also argue that tertiary education is a sign of dedication and commitment, as it requires significant time, effort, and financial investment. Without this investment, they suggest, individuals may not be able to reach their full potential in their careers.

Opponents of tertiary education, however, argue that it is an unnecessary expense and time commitment. They argue that there are many other ways to acquire the skills and knowledge needed to succeed in the workforce, such as vocational training, apprenticeships, or internships. They also suggest that the cost of tertiary education is too high, and the debt incurred can outweigh the potential benefits. Additionally, they argue that some fields, such as entrepreneurship, require creativity and innovation that cannot necessarily be taught in a classroom setting.

Despite these arguments, it is worth noting that tertiary education can provide numerous benefits beyond just career success. For instance, it can provide opportunities for personal growth and development, exposure to new ideas and perspectives, and the chance to make connections with others in a chosen field.

To sum up, while the necessity of tertiary education is a subject of debate, it is important to recognize that there are many different paths to success. Individuals should consider their own unique circumstances, goals, and interests when deciding whether to pursue tertiary education or explore other options. Regardless of the chosen path, dedication, commitment, and hard work are key to achieving success in any field.

The Pros and Cons of Making All New Cars Electric

As the world looks for ways to reduce its carbon footprint and slow down climate change, there has been increasing interest in electric cars as a more sustainable alternative to gas-powered vehicles. Some people argue that making all new cars electric is the best way to achieve this goal. However, there are pros and cons to this approach, and it is important to consider both sides of the argument.

On the one hand, making all new cars electric could have significant environmental benefits. Electric cars produce zero emissions and are much more energy-efficient than gas-powered vehicles. By replacing gas cars with electric ones, we could drastically reduce our greenhouse gas emissions and slow down the rate of climate change. In addition, electric cars are much quieter than traditional cars and have a lower cost of ownership in the long run, since they require less maintenance and fuel costs.

On the other hand, there are several challenges that need to be addressed before making all new cars electric. One of the biggest challenges is the cost. Electric cars are still significantly more expensive than gas-powered cars, and many people cannot afford them. In addition, the infrastructure to support electric cars, such as charging stations, is still not as widespread as gas stations. This means that electric car owners may have difficulty finding a charging station when they need one. Moreover, the production of electric car batteries requires significant amounts of energy and resources, and the disposal of these batteries can have environmental impacts as well.

To conclude, making all new cars electric is a complex issue with both benefits and challenges. While it could have significant environmental benefits, there are also economic and infrastructural challenges that need to be addressed before this can become a reality. Ultimately, it will be up to governments, automakers, and consumers to work together to determine whether the benefits of electric cars outweigh the costs, and whether a shift to all-electric cars is the best way to move forward in a more sustainable future.

The Pros and Cons of Artificial Intelligence in Today's World

Artificial intelligence (AI) has become increasingly prominent in today's society, with new applications emerging every day. While some people believe that AI will be a driving force for positive change, others are more sceptical and see it as a threat to human well-being. This essay will explore both sides of the argument to determine whether AI will ultimately help or hurt the world.

On the one hand, AI has the potential to revolutionize many industries, from healthcare to transportation. It can make medical diagnoses more accurate, assist with complex surgeries, and streamline the drug development process. In the transportation sector, self-driving cars could reduce accidents and traffic congestion. Additionally, AI can help to reduce labour costs and increase efficiency in many areas, which could lead to lower prices for consumers.

On the other hand, there are many concerns about the potential negative impact of AI on society. One concern is that AI could displace millions of workers, particularly in industries such as manufacturing and transportation. Another concern is that AI could be used to create autonomous weapons, which could make warfare more deadly and unpredictable. Additionally, there are worries that AI could be used to spread disinformation, as deepfakes and other AI-generated media become more sophisticated.

While there are valid arguments on both sides, it is difficult to predict whether AI will ultimately help or hurt the world. It will largely depend on how society chooses to use this technology. It is important for policymakers and developers to carefully consider the potential impact of AI on society, and to put in place measures to mitigate any negative effects. This could include investing in retraining programs for displaced workers, implementing regulations around the development and use of autonomous weapons, and working to prevent the spread of disinformation.

In conclusion, while AI has the potential to bring about many positive changes, there are also valid concerns about the impact of this technology on society. It is up to individuals and society as a whole to ensure that AI is used responsibly and ethically, in a way that benefits humanity as a whole. By carefully weighing the pros and cons of AI and taking steps to address any negative effects, we can work towards a future in which this technology is a force for good.

The Emotional Differences between Men and Women

The debate about whether men and women are equally emotional has been a topic of discussion for years. There are some who believe that men are less emotional than women, while others argue that both genders experience emotions in different ways. While there may be some differences in the way men and women express their emotions, there is evidence to suggest that both genders are equally emotional.

One reason why people may believe that men are less emotional than women is due to cultural norms and expectations. Men are often taught to be tough, stoic, and to suppress their emotions. This can lead to the perception that men do not experience emotions as deeply as women do. However, this cultural expectation is changing, and more men are beginning to express their emotions openly.

Another reason why some people may believe that men are less emotional is that they tend to express their emotions differently than women. Men are more likely to express their emotions through action, while women are more likely to express their emotions verbally. This can lead to the perception that men are less emotional, when in reality, they are simply expressing their emotions in a different way.

Studies have shown that men and women experience emotions in similar ways. For example, research has found that both men and women experience the same range of emotions, including happiness, sadness, anger, and fear. Additionally, studies have found that both men and women experience the same intensity of emotions.

However, while men and women may experience emotions in similar ways, there are some differences in the way they express their emotions. Men tend to express their emotions through actions, such as playing sports, working out, or fixing things around the house. Women, on the other hand, tend to express their emotions through verbal communication, such as talking with friends or family members.

To conclude, while there are differences in the way that men and women express their emotions, there is evidence to suggest that both genders are equally emotional. Cultural expectations and norms may lead to the perception that men are less emotional, but this is changing as more men express their emotions openly. Ultimately, the expression of emotions is a personal choice, and everyone should be free to express their emotions in the way that feels most comfortable for them.

The Benefits and Drawbacks of Space Exploration

Space exploration has been a topic of fascination for decades. With advancements in technology, scientists have been able to study and explore the mysteries of space more than ever before. However, the question remains whether space exploration is worth the resources and funding invested in it. Some argue that space exploration is a waste of resources, while others believe that it has numerous benefits.

One of the biggest advantages of space exploration is the scientific knowledge that we can gain. By studying the planets, stars, and other celestial bodies, we can learn more about our universe and the laws of physics that govern it. This knowledge can lead to new discoveries and advancements in fields such as medicine, energy, and technology. For example, the technology used in space exploration has led to innovations such as GPS and satellite communication.

Another benefit of space exploration is its potential economic benefits. The exploration of space can create new industries and job opportunities. For instance, space tourism is a growing industry, and companies like SpaceX are working to create affordable space travel. Additionally, the resources found in space, such as rare metals and minerals, can be used to create new technologies and generate economic growth.

On the other hand, some argue that the cost of space exploration outweighs its benefits. The amount of resources and funding that goes into space exploration could be used to solve problems here on Earth, such as poverty, climate change, and healthcare. Additionally, the risks associated with space travel, such as accidents and radiation exposure, are not worth the potential benefits.

Despite the debate surrounding space exploration, it is important to continue to explore our universe. Space exploration allows us to expand our knowledge, create new industries, and potentially solve some of the world's biggest problems. However, it is essential to consider the costs and benefits of space exploration carefully and ensure that the funding allocated to it is used effectively.

Given these points, space exploration has its advantages and disadvantages. While some may argue that it is not worth the investment, the potential benefits are too significant to ignore. As we continue to learn more about space and the technology advances, we must consider the ethical and economic implications of space exploration to ensure that it is done responsibly and for the greater good.

Should Internships Be Paid: A Discussion on Fair Compensation for Interns

Internships are often seen as an opportunity to gain valuable work experience and build connections in a particular field. However, the question of whether internships should be paid or unpaid is a controversial one. On the one hand, unpaid internships are often criticized for being exploitative and taking advantage of young people. On the other hand, some argue that internships are a form of on-the-job training and that interns are receiving valuable experience that will benefit them in the future.

Those who argue in favour of paid internships point to the fact that many internships require a significant amount of work and effort, and that interns are often performing tasks that are essential to the functioning of the organization. These tasks may include answering phones, scheduling appointments, or conducting research. If the organization were to hire someone to perform these tasks, they would likely have to pay that person a salary. Therefore, it seems unfair to expect interns to do this work for free.

Additionally, those who support paid internships argue that unpaid internships are often only accessible to students who come from wealthy families or who have other sources of financial support. This means that many talented and hardworking students are unable to take advantage of these opportunities simply because they cannot afford to work for free. This creates a situation where the people who are able to get internships and gain valuable experience are not necessarily the most qualified or talented, but rather the ones who have the most financial resources.

On the other hand, some argue that internships are a form of on-the-job training and that interns are receiving valuable experience that will benefit them in the future. They argue that internships should be seen as an investment in one's future career, and that the experience gained during an internship is worth the time and effort put into it. Furthermore, some argue that the cost of hiring and training interns may be too high for some organizations, particularly small businesses or non-profit organizations.

However, while it is true that some internships provide valuable experience, it is important to remember that internships are not a substitute for paid work. Interns should not be expected to perform essential tasks without fair compensation. Unpaid internships can be exploitative and limit opportunities for those who cannot afford to work for free. It is important to ensure that all interns are fairly compensated for their time and effort.

To sum up, internships' compensation is a complex issue. While some argue that internships provide valuable on-the-job training and should not necessarily be paid, it is important to recognize that interns are often performing essential tasks and that unpaid internships can be exploitative. Therefore, all internships should be fairly compensated, ensuring that talented and hardworking students from all backgrounds have access to these valuable opportunities.

The Pros and Cons of a Woke Culture

The term "woke" has become increasingly popular in recent years, with more and more people advocating for social and political awareness. However, some argue that this "woke culture" has gone too far, while others maintain that it is necessary for progress. So, is woke culture necessary?

One of the main arguments in favour of a woke culture is that it brings attention to important issues, such as racism, sexism, and other forms of discrimination. By highlighting these issues, it encourages individuals and institutions to take action and create positive change. Additionally, it creates a more inclusive environment where everyone is accepted and valued, regardless of their race, gender, or sexual orientation.

On the other hand, some argue that a woke culture can go too far and lead to unnecessary outrage and division. It can create an environment where individuals are afraid to express their opinions, even if they are well-intentioned, for fear of being labelled as "ignorant" or "bigoted." Moreover, some argue that woke culture can lead to a cancel culture, where individuals or institutions are boycotted or ostracized for holding certain views or making mistakes.

In conclusion, a woke culture has its benefits and drawbacks. While it can bring attention to important issues and create a more inclusive environment, it can also lead to unnecessary outrage and division. Therefore, it is important to strike a balance and create a society that encourages open and respectful dialogue, while also recognizing and addressing issues of discrimination and inequality.

The Relevance of Feminism in Today's Society

In recent years, the topic of feminism has been widely debated, with some arguing that it is no longer relevant in modern society. However, the reality is that there is still a long way to go in achieving gender equality, and feminism remains an important movement to help achieve this goal.

Despite progress in some areas, such as women's increased participation in the workforce and greater representation in politics, women continue to face challenges that are unique to their gender. For example, women still earn less than men for doing the same job, and are underrepresented in many high-paying fields such as science, technology, engineering, and math (STEM). Additionally, women face a greater risk of violence and harassment, both in public and in their homes.

Feminism is important because it seeks to address these issues and advocate for gender equality in all areas of life. Feminism encourages women to recognize and assert their rights, and it calls on men to become allies in the fight for equality. Furthermore, it is important to acknowledge that the benefits of feminism extend beyond gender, as it helps to create a more just and equitable society for all.

While some argue that feminism is no longer necessary, citing the progress that has been made, the reality is that gender inequality still exists in many areas. As such, the need for feminism remains important and relevant in today's society.

All in all, feminism is a necessary and relevant movement in modern society. It serves to address issues of gender inequality and advocate for women's rights, while also promoting a more just and equitable society for all. While progress has been made in some areas, there is still much work to be done to achieve true gender equality, and feminism remains an important force in this fight.

Online Degrees vs. Traditional Degrees: Which is More Legitimate?

As technology advances, more and more universities are offering online degrees. While the convenience of studying from anywhere at any time is appealing, many are still sceptical about the value of these degrees compared to traditional brick-and-mortar institutions. The question arises: Is a degree from an online college as legitimate as a degree from a brick-and-mortar school?

There are several arguments on both sides of this issue. On the one hand, online degrees are becoming increasingly popular due to their accessibility and flexibility. Online programs allow students to attend class from anywhere with an internet connection and offer more flexible scheduling options. For individuals who are unable to attend traditional classes, such as those with work or family obligations, online programs can provide an opportunity to further their education.

However, others argue that online degrees are not as legitimate as those obtained through traditional institutions. Online degrees may lack the same level of rigor and academic standards as their brick-and-mortar counterparts, and some employers may view them as less valuable. Additionally, online programs may not provide the same level of networking opportunities and face-to-face interactions with professors and classmates.

Ultimately, the legitimacy of an online degree depends on the institution offering it and the quality of the program. Some online programs are just as rigorous and reputable as traditional ones, while others may not be up to par. It is important for prospective students to thoroughly research and evaluate the quality of the program, the institution's accreditation, and the reputation of the degree.

As a conclusion, the question of whether a degree from an online college is as legitimate as a degree from a brick-and-mortar school is a complex issue. While online programs offer accessibility and flexibility, they may not always provide the same level of academic rigor and networking opportunities. It is important for prospective students to carefully evaluate the quality of the program and institution before pursuing an online degree.

Who is Responsible for Children's Obesity: Parents or Manufacturers?

Childhood obesity has become a major health issue in many countries around the world. With the rise of processed and high-calorie foods, coupled with a sedentary lifestyle, children are becoming increasingly overweight and unhealthy. While there are many factors that contribute to childhood obesity, two parties are often held accountable: parents and food manufacturers.

Parents play a vital role in their children's health and well-being, including their dietary habits. As such, many argue that it is primarily the responsibility of parents to ensure that their children eat a healthy and balanced diet. Parents are the ones who decide what their children eat, where they eat, and how much they eat. They are responsible for teaching their children about healthy eating habits and the importance of physical activity.

However, some argue that it is unfair to place all the blame on parents. Food manufacturers also play a significant role in the prevalence of childhood obesity. They often create and market unhealthy products that are high in calories, sugar, and fat. These products are designed to be appealing to children, often featuring bright colours, cartoon characters, and other attention-grabbing features. Additionally, food manufacturers may not always provide clear and accurate information about the nutritional content of their products, making it difficult for parents to make informed decisions about what to feed their children.

Ultimately, both parents and food manufacturers have a role to play in combating childhood obesity. Parents should prioritize their children's health and make an effort to provide them with healthy, balanced meals. They should also limit their children's consumption of unhealthy, processed foods and encourage physical activity. At the same time, food manufacturers should be held accountable for the products they create and market, and they should be required to provide clear and accurate information about their nutritional content.

In a nutshell, the issue of childhood obesity is a complex one, and both parents and food manufacturers must take responsibility for it. While parents are ultimately responsible for their children's health, food manufacturers also play a significant role in the foods that are available to children. By working together, parents and food manufacturers can help to combat childhood obesity and promote healthier habits for future generations.

Mandatory Vaccination: The Key to Public Health

In recent years, there has been a growing controversy surrounding the issue of mandatory vaccination. Some individuals argue that requiring vaccines infringes on their personal freedom, while others maintain that it is necessary for the safety and well-being of the public as a whole. Despite the differing opinions, it is clear that mandatory vaccination is essential for preventing the spread of infectious diseases and protecting the health of society.

One of the primary arguments in favour of mandatory vaccination is the need to protect vulnerable populations, such as the elderly, children, and immunocompromised individuals. These individuals are more susceptible to infections and are at a higher risk of experiencing severe complications or death from diseases like the flu, measles, and whooping cough. By ensuring that everyone is vaccinated, we can create herd immunity, which effectively stops the spread of the disease and provides a buffer to protect those who cannot receive vaccines themselves.

Another argument in favour of mandatory vaccination is the need to prevent disease outbreaks. Vaccines have been instrumental in reducing the incidence of infectious diseases like polio, smallpox, and measles, which once caused widespread illness and death. However, as seen in recent outbreaks of measles and other diseases, not all individuals are receiving the necessary vaccinations. This lack of compliance not only puts the individuals themselves at risk, but it also creates the potential for disease outbreaks that can impact the health of the broader community.

Despite the clear benefits of mandatory vaccination, some individuals argue that it infringes on their personal freedom and right to make decisions about their own health. However, it is important to note that individual choice does not exist in a vacuum. The decision to not vaccinate not only puts the individual at risk, but also has the potential to harm others in the community. Moreover, mandatory vaccination laws do not take away the individual's right to choose whether or not to vaccinate, but rather require them to take responsibility for their decision by facing the consequences of not being vaccinated, such as being excluded from public spaces and facing potential consequences if they spread the disease to others.

In conclusion, mandatory vaccination is an essential component of public health. It protects vulnerable populations, prevents the spread of infectious diseases, and ensures that individuals take responsibility for their health decisions. While it is important to respect individual choice, it is equally important to prioritize the safety and health of the community as a whole. By requiring vaccinations for all individuals, we can work towards creating a healthier and safer society for everyone.

Are you struggling to write a great
argumentative essay for your
IELTS or TOEFL exam?

Look no further!

"101 Must-Read Argumentative Essays" is a straightforward
guide to help you succeed.

This comprehensive book is packed with 101 carefully crafted essays
that cover a wide range of topics. Each essay is accompanied by
a breakdown of its structure and content, giving you the tools you
need to write a winning essay. With "101 Must-Read Argumentative Essays,"
you'll have everything you need to achieve the highest score on your exam.
"101 Must-Read Argumentative Essays" - the no-nonsense and affordable
solution to help you succeed.

| Page